CELEBRATION

THE STORY OF A TOWN

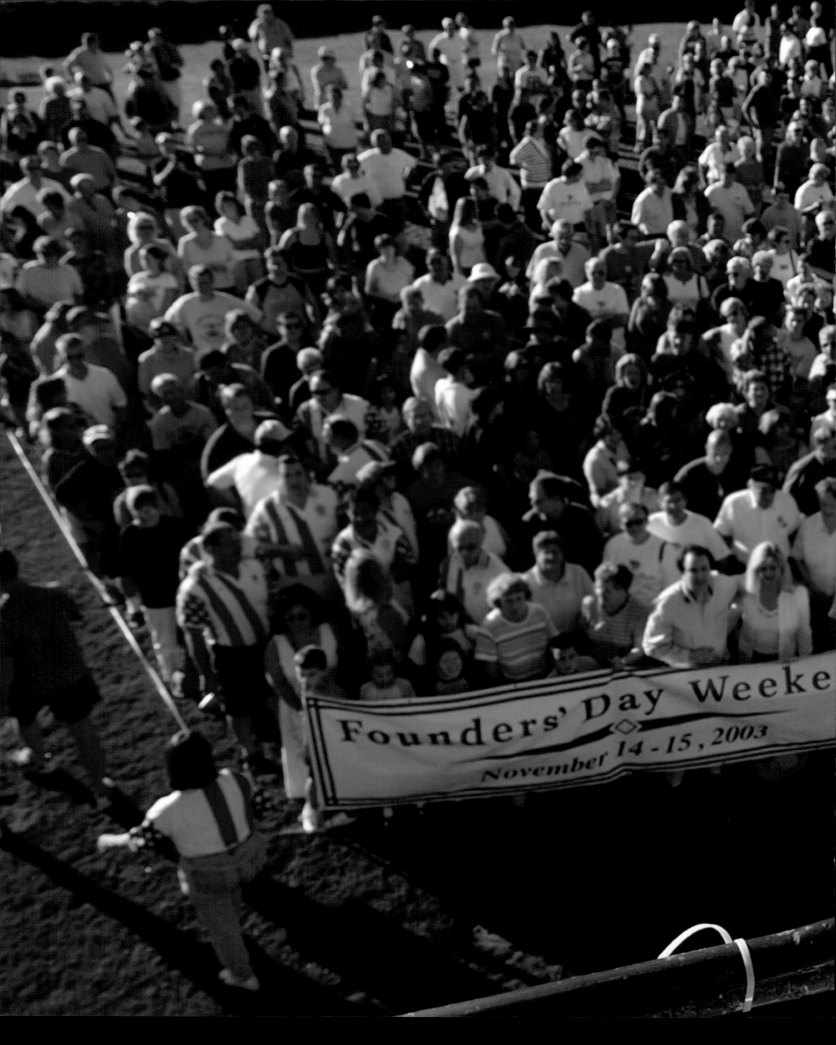

Founders' Day Weeke
November 14 - 15, 2003

INTRODUCTION BY JAQUELIN T. ROBERTSON AND ROBERT A.M. STERN

CELEB

THE STORY

A ROUNDTABLE PRESS BOOK

RATION
OF A TOWN

BY MICHAEL LASSELL

Disney
EDITIONS
New York

A Roundtable Press Book
New York

EDITIONS
New York

Printed in China

For information address Disney Editions, 114 Fifth Avenue, New York, NY 10011.

For Disney Editions
Editorial Director: Wendy Lefkon
Editor: Jody Revenson

For Roundtable Press, Inc.
Directors: Marsha Melnick, Julie Merberg
Design: Jon Glick, mouse+tiger
Editor: John Glenn

Photo and Illustration Credits
Credits are indicated by page number and letters. From top to bottom, t stands for top, c for center,
and b for bottom. From left to right, l stands for left, m for middle, and r for right.

Peter Aaron/ESTO: 52. **Mark Ashman:** front cover (tl, br); 4–7 (all); 11 (l, mr, r); 13; 36 (all); 55 (t); 63 (br); 65 (all); 67 (b); 70; 76 (tl);
76–77 (bl); 81–83 (all); 84 (t, bl, br); 85 (bl); 86–87 (all); 88 (bl, br); 89; 90 (tl, bl); 92–93 (all); 95 (r); 98–99 (all); 103–104 (all); 107 (t);
108 (tl, tr, cl, cr); 109 (b); 110; 111 (bl, br); 112–115 (all); 116 (tl, b); 120–121 (all); 122 (b); 124–125 (all); 127 (m, r); 128–132 (all);
134–136 (all); 138–139 (all); 142–143 (tl, tm, tr, bl); 149; 151; 154–155 (all); 160. **Gary Bogdon:** 2–3; 11 (ml, m); 12 (bl, br); 14; 16–17
(b); 35 (b); 58–59; 60 (b); 68–69 (all); 76–77 (tm); 77 (tr); 79 (all); 84 (bm); 85 (br); 88 (t); 90 (cl); 90–91; 94; 95 (l, m); 96–97 (all);
100–102 (all); 105 (all); 107 (b); 108 (b); 109 (t); 115 (tl, tr); 116 (tr); 117–119 (all); 122 (t); 123; 126; 127 (l); 133; 137; 144–145 (all);
150; 153. **Chris Cary:** 57; 63 (bl). **The Celebration Company:** back cover; 56 (t); 66; 85 (t); 146. **Cooper Robertson & Partners:** 38–39
(background). **© Disney:** front cover (tr); 18–19 (all); 21–24 (all); 26; 30–31 (all); 35 (t); 37; 42 (all); 44–49 (all); 51; 54; 62–63 (t); 64;
74–75. **Michael Graves & Associates:** 12 (tr); 38 (tl); 53 (b). **Philip Johnson, Ritchie & Fiore, Architects:** front cover (bl); 50 (all).
Gary Krueger Photography: 53 (t). **John Mason for Robert A.M. Stern Architects:** 32 (tr, bl). **Michael McCann:** 12 (tl); 16–17 (background);
17 (tr); 41; 43; 71–72 (all); 76–77 (background); 142–143 (background). **Moore/Andersson Architects, Inc.:** 55 (b). **© James R. Morse NYC:**
74 (b). **Cesar Pelli & Associates:** 56 (b). **Aldo Rossi Studio di Architettura:** 39 (t). **Lynn Sands:** 11 (t). **Roger Sherman:** 28; 60 (t); 60–61;
140–141. **Smith Aerial Photos:** 16 (t); 38–39 (b); 67 (t); 78; 80 (all). *Southern Living:* 106. **Robert A.M. Stern Architects:** 32 (tl, br); 34.
Venturi, Scott Brown & Associates: 62 (b).

ISBN 0-7868-5405-7

First Edition

2 4 6 8 10 9 7 5 3 1

"By nature, I'm an experimenter."

—*Walt Disney*

This book is dedicated to

the people of Celebration

for their extravagant hospitality

and to everyone who took a risk

to make Celebration happen

CONTENTS

INTRODUCTION

Celebration is a traditional American town built anew. While this sounds relatively straightforward and benign, many of our concepts were contrary to most all conventional contemporary thought about community development. The skeptics were vocal, and we often found ourselves defending this "new town" concept long before the first dirt was turned. But our vision and the commitment of the "town" founders was strong.

Celebration draws on and celebrates the best ideas found in the best, and best–loved, American places, villages, and towns, from Nantucket and East Hampton to Charleston and Coral Gables, practical places filled with ideas that for over three centuries have shaped our lives and value systems, and remain relevant and vital today. Celebration deals with schools and churches, libraries and banks, office buildings, shops, houses, and playing fields in a cohesive and interconnected way; it encourages walking and biking, domesticates the car, protects wetlands, and reestablishes the street as our central public setting and public parks as a focal point for residential life. In its village center, there are apartments over the shops; a cinema, restaurants, and a grocery store all just across the street. Celebration is both a new and a familiar place, a place that people want to live and work in as well as visit.

Now, ten years since the project was first announced, Celebration is a success. It is an important benchmark for future community design, a convincing demonstration that it is possible to make and market a town. Celebration was undertaken with high ideals by its developer, The Walt Disney Company, whose leader Michael D. Eisner pushed for its realization as a business proposition that also needed to make a contribution to the quality of American life. Celebration's goals of livability, sustainability, and strong community spirit resonate with a wide range of important audiences: consumers, educators, government officials, policy-makers, and health-care professionals.

In years to come, the names of the architects and the planners of Celebration will probably be forgotten by many. But the town will stand as a rare testimony to the enduring tradition and appeal of American towns.

Jaquelin Robertson
Robert A.M. Stern

1. IMAGINING

A TOWN

"It all began with a mouse," Walt Disney was fond of saying of his ever-growing international entertainment conglomerate, although, in fact, Disney's own career predated Mickey's by nearly a decade. But the mouse made the man a household name along with his own, which would have been "Mortimer" had Lillian, Walt's wife, not intervened. Without Mickey there would have been no Disneyland and without Disneyland no town called Celebration in the northwestern reaches of central Florida's Osceola County.

Among the most interesting aspects of the Walt Disney myth is how far it misses the man, even in his professional life. Widely seen as an animator who somehow got involved in live-action films and then amusement parks, the truth is that Walt, as he was universally known, started his own animation studio hoping to move to Hollywood some day to direct live-action movies.

This was typical of Walt, whose imagination, by all accounts, looked to the long view and the big picture. Furthermore, Walter Elias Disney had always been fascinated by the ways in which real people actually live. It is no accident that the first thing one sees at Disneyland (as well as its cousins in Orlando, Paris, and Tokyo) is Main Street, U.S.A. This romanticized re-creation of the central downtown street of Marceline, Missouri, where Walt did most of his growing up, has become an internationally recognized manifestation of an ideal but bygone period in the American good life.

"He loved...nostalgia," says Walt Disney Imagineering executive Marty Sklar in *Walt: The Man Behind the Myth,* Katherine and Richard Greene's formidable documentary film, and "he loved technology."

"I don't believe there's a challenge anywhere in the world that's more important to people everywhere than finding solutions to the problems of our communities." —*Walt Disney*

Walt Disney in front of City Hall at Disneyland (ABOVE) and an artist's rendition of Main Street, U.S.A., an idealized version of the Disney family's Missouri hometown (BELOW).

Consequently, from his earliest notions of Disneyland in the late 1940s, Walt had his eye on a higher goal than his obvious talent to amuse. He wanted to make a palpable difference in the way Americans existed every day, not just in the way they were occasionally entertained. And if he was a man with one foot planted oaklike in the gauzy days of yore and yesteryear, the other was clearly striding or blasting off—Colossus-like—toward a rocket-fueled future. It was a future that Walt wanted to help create.

MAIN ST. U.S.A.

In writing about Disneyland in 2001, Paul Goldberger, the widely respected architecture critic for the *New Yorker*, expounded on some of the social currents that gave rise to Disneyland and, ultimately, to the creation of Celebration:

"Walt Disney realized before anybody else," Goldberger wrote, "that, while much was gained in the sort of new suburban automobile-landscape of southern California, something critical was lost. That was the experience of urbanism—being in a public place, where you walk around, see other people, and enjoy this wonderful combination of security and surprise.... That whole element of a traditional village had just disappeared with people going in their cars on freeways and sitting in little tracts, and not connecting in the way they once did."

This feeling of disconnection is one of the defining characteristics of the twentieth century, and the sprawling housing developments of the 1950s and 1960s with vast expanses of identical starter homes did not help mitigate the pervasive angst. In fact, these mazes of carbon-copy Cape Cods became a broadly lampooned but very real symbol of dehumanization. In countless comic strips of the 1950s, hapless husbands would return from a hard day's work only to walk in on their neighbors at dinner—or some more intimate activity—since each house looked so much like the one next door.

What Paul Goldberger saw in Disneyland was a hint of the remedy that would, in the 1980s and 1990s—when the first generation of post-Disneyland architects was reaching maturity—give rise to the so-called New Urbanist movement. It was axiomatic of this move back into town centers (literally and figuratively) that humans, being social creatures by nature, had a fundamental longing to interact with their neighbors. If you took away this routine interaction, the post-suburban wisdom ran, the social fabric would not hold. And, indeed, the ravaged American cities of the 1960s and 1970s seemed dismal enough proof.

By the 1980s, many perfectly viable downtowns in cities across America had been all but abandoned for the exurbs by the middle- and even working-class families that had supported them. Happily, however, a crop of forward-looking architects, planners, and developers began to look to the past as a way of repairing the unraveling present. These activist professionals began to reclaim old inner-city neighborhoods in attractive ways—restoring essential street life with independent retail shops and small restaurants that created traffic, activity, and greater intercourse, hence increased safety and local pride.

Additionally, young families began to follow loft-converting artists back to disused industrial sectors—urban frontiers—not so much in quest of space or light, but searching for some of the traditional, lost verities of small-town living. These New Urbanist pioneers, reversing suburban flight, were settling down within a short distance (often walking or biking distance) from downtown work, shopping, and entertainment venues.

Disneyland opened at the height of America's flight to sprawling suburbs, but prescient architects pointed out that Main Street, U.S.A.—despite its fantasy Victorian facade—anticipated real solutions for communities of the future.

Simultaneously, and out of a similar impulse, purpose-built towns were attempting to recapture a greater sense of community than had been typical of the cookie-cutter housing epitomized by the first Levittown. One of the first and most successful of these so-called New Towns (or neotraditional towns, as they are alternately called) was the resort enclave of Seaside. Built on 80 acres of Gulf-fronting land on the Florida panhandle, Seaside was the defining project of visionary husband-and-wife architect/planners Andrés Duany and Elizabeth Plater-Zyberk. In Seaside, the public-minded designers set out to create a cohesive community that had as its virtues some of the same qualities Paul Goldberger found in Disneyland:

"The shopping mall, town square, and entertainment zone were combined for the first time in Disneyland. The idea that you could combine a return to that experience with entertainment was pretty dazzling.... [Since] Disneyland opened, we've seen the real city and the theme park become more and more alike. Cities are less necessary economically because we don't need them to do business the way we once did. By and large, cities have survived by becoming places of entertainment, which means that real cities have become more like Disneyland."

More recently, the Disney company has begun to face these same issues in major cities. In the late 1980s and into the 1990s, Disney played a pivotal role in the redevelopment and resuscitation of Hollywood Boulevard and of Forty-second Street in New York. In fact, both stretches of real estate have turned Mean Streets, in the parlance of Raymond Chandler, to something much more like Main Street (or, as critics suggest, a mall). Both these former combat zones were once known primarily for drug dealing, prostitution, and XXX-rated movies; they are now almost entirely devoted to family entertainment. On both coasts, the early participation of Disney (in restoring the New Amsterdam Theatre in New York and the El Capitan in Hollywood) provided anchoring reassurance to other developers.

These forays into urban renewal are not, however, aberrations of latter-day Disney executives who had strayed somehow from Walt Disney's original vision. James Rouse, the revolutionary urban planner who created the paradigmatic town of Columbia, Maryland, claimed in the 1960s that Disneyland was "the outstanding piece of urban design in the United States." In fact, Disney himself had much more elaborate magic up his sorcerer's sleeve. At the time of his death in 1966, Walt was deeply engaged in planning to build a city of his own.

The world knows that, as night follows day, Walt Disney World followed Disneyland. Axiomatic to common knowledge is that Disneyland was so successful that Walt simply decided to expand—hardly surprising, but far from visionary as business plans go. The mustachioed animator, however, was no ordinary businessman. As it happens, when Walt went shopping for an east-of-the-Mississippi site for what would become the most popular tourist destination on earth, he had already decided to turn most of the entertainment work of his company over to others. He was about to embark on what he considered his real life's work.

"The Florida project," as it became known inside the Disney company, would include a Magic Kingdom theme park, but only as a lure, as a taste of the familiar for the legions that loved the Mouse. What Walt really had in mind was something grander, newer, and of more enduring importance than anything he had ever done before. And that project, which had long been percolating in his active imagination, was a City of the Future. Walt called his dream EPCOT, an acronym for Experimental Prototype Community of Tomorrow.

Epcot was a futuristic fantasy based on sound principles of contemporary planning that came from such thinkers as modernist giant Le Corbusier, among others, who set the stage for what became "serious" architecture and design throughout the twentieth century. As recorded at the online Disney Family Museum, "Walt imagined Epcot as a real city, in which tens of thousands of people could work and live—and enjoy the latest technologies produced by American corporations."

"He'd talk for hours about the houses and how the kids would go to school," recalled Marc Davis, a Disney designer (animator of such characters as Tinker Bell and Cruella De Vil, and Walt's nephew by marriage). "He'd even talk for hours about garbage disposal. He was really engrossed in it."

Walt Disney shows off plans for his "Florida project."

AIR CONDITIONED COMMERCIAL CENTER

ARCADE

TRANSPORTATION

MONORAIL

LOBBY

W.D. WAY

INTERNATIONAL SHOPPING & DINING

ARCADE

OFFICES ETC.

APTS.

TO COMMERCIAL & SERVICE AREAS

AUTOS
TRUCKS
TRUCKS
AUTOS

MONORAIL

OVER PASS

SCHOOLS

FIRE

FIRE

CHURCHES

SCHOOL

W.D. WAY

LITTLE LEAGUE BALL ETC.

G. E. COMPUTERIZED ELEVATED ELECTRIC CART TRACK

TENNIS-SWIMMING-ETC.

W.D. WAY

TYP. 4
G.E. ELECTRIC CART
ENTRANCE & EXIT TO
G.E. COMPUTERIZED TRK.

RESIDENTIAL   AREAS

COLLECTOR ROAD

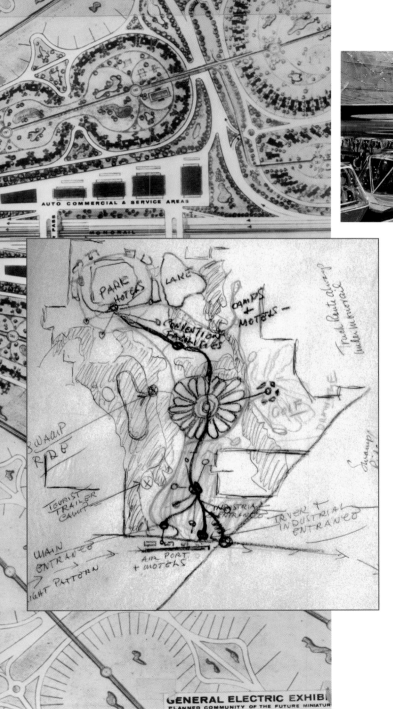

The megametropolis would radiate out from a central hub that contained the towering glass-and-steel commercial and entertainment core. Transportation would include a network of people movers and high-speed monorails to outlying residential zones. (Walt, a train enthusiast, had his own one-eighth-scale steam train at home—big enough for adults to ride—and built America's first functional monorail at Disneyland.) Housing at Epcot, freestanding homes as well as apartment complexes, would be set in well-planted green spaces alive with parks and lakes for family outings.

In 1965, the company Walt built bought 27,433 acres of Florida land in Orange and Osceola counties for approximately $5 million (about $200 an acre). The tract was twice the size of Manhattan and 150 times the size of Disneyland back in Anaheim, California. Acquired quietly to prevent the price of the land from skyrocketing should Disney's interest become public knowledge, the land would soon be transformed, as would life in Central Florida.

Although Disney's property is located in the heart of Central Florida, in 1965 it was many miles from the nearest community or center of local government. There was no available infrastructure or tax base that could even begin to support Disney's vast plans for the property. The Florida legislature stepped in and established Reedy Creek Improvement District (RCID) in 1967. The state granted RCID privileges that were needed to plan and develop Disney's property, including the right to float bonds and build infrastructure.

Walt's original sketch of the plan for his visionary Experimental Prototype Community of Tomorrow (EPCOT) inspired waves of meticulously detailed plans and renderings for a radiating, high-tech city worthy of Jules Verne.

When Walt died in December 1966, ten days after his sixty-fifth birthday, ground had not yet even been broken for the Florida project. It was left to his lifelong business partner, elder brother Roy O. Disney, who had been planning to retire, to carry the project forward. Roy Disney himself died just months after the opening of Walt Disney World's Magic Kingdom in 1971.

A second theme park, called Epcot, opened eleven years later, in 1982, but it was a mere shadow of the map of tomorrow that Walt said he saw on the ceiling of his hospital room as he lay dying of lung cancer years earlier. Although a far cry from Walt's jet-propelled fantasy, Epcot remains the venue for considering the natural history of our planet as well as vanguard technology.

The Epcot that opened in 1982
was not a city but a theme park.

By the early 1980s, Disney was suffering something of an identity crisis—or at least a fiscal one. The company had been, it is widely agreed, resting on its creative laurels and on the legacy of its prime mover in the period following the Disney brothers' deaths, and its position was far from secure. The reliable hordes of visitors to Disneyland and Walt Disney World were beginning to thin; Disney films were routinely dismissed by critics as irrelevant and ignored by ticket buyers.

Worse, the financial standing of the company made it vulnerable to the prowling corporate raiders whose piratical takeovers set the tone for doing business in the 1980s.

But in 1984, after a protracted search and negotiation, a nervous Disney corporation hired entertainment industry shaker Michael Eisner as its chairman and chief executive officer (along with Frank Wells, who would serve as the company's president). Eisner would be the creative head, Wells the money man. The new team's mandate was to revive the company's flagging motion picture business and invigorate theme park attendance. Additionally, they were charged, although the term was not then in common parlance, with extending and maximizing the Disney brand—one of the most recognizable, respected, and powerful on earth—and maximizing its corporate assets.

As part of their new duties, Eisner and Wells (who was killed in a helicopter accident in 1994) turned their analytical eyes to every aspect of the company, including its real estate. Did Disney really need all that property outside of Orlando? Some even felt that the failure to exploit this asset in the sonic economy of the 1980s was one of the things that attracted corporate raiders.

The task of evaluating the real estate fell to Peter Rummell at Disney Development Company. DDC was later realigned and is now part of what makes up Walt Disney Imagineering (a clever corporate neologism that combines creative imagination with practical engineering).

"It was a two-tiered process," remembers Rummell, who now runs the enormous St. Joe development firm from Jacksonville, Florida. "First we undertook a massive planning study of all 27,000 acres, trying to think about every possible way in anyone's wildest imagination the core business, the resort/theme park business, could grow." It was determined by a complex formula with innumerable factors that the long-range build-out plan for The Walt Disney World Resort would extend to a maximum of five theme parks and around fifty thousand hotel rooms, about twenty thousand more than existed at the time. (Disney-MGM Studios, which opened in 1989, and Disney's Animal Kingdom, which opened in 1998, brought the current number of theme parks at Disney World to four.)

"The second step," Rummell instructs, "was to take that density and plan it, to see—once we had built all that, and allowed for a green buffer zone—if there was anything left. And the conclusion was that we could do all of that building and still stay north of 192."

U.S. 192, a high-density commercial strip that targets a transient tourist market, is only one of the main roads that traverses the Disney property in Florida. It is also sliced in two unequal parts by Interstate 4, which runs generally northeast from Tampa on the Gulf Coast to Daytona Beach on the Atlantic. There is, additionally, the Central Florida Greenway, SR-417. About 20,000 acres of Walt's original parcel, on which all the theme parks, hotels, vacation clubs, and other resort attractions now operate, is north and west of these major arteries. The large majority of the land lies in Orange County, the seat of which is the city of Orlando.

An additional 10,000 acres—no small spread—lies to the south and east of the parks, most of it below U.S. 192, in Osceola County. Some of this "land" was, in fact, wetlands, although much had long served the region's cattle industry. While tourism was the business of Orange County, Osceola was farm- and ranchland, and the number of cows and horses there far exceeded its human population. Osceola County was—and still is—home to many of the low- and moderate-wage earners that were employed by the region's many tourist attractions. What would Disney do?

"We certainly thought of selling the land off," remembers Eisner of the 10,000 undeveloped Florida acres. "But my feeling was that it wasn't the right strategy, because we would wind up with low-end, unexciting, uncreative development. . . . What I wanted to do was to put something south of the resort that would encourage other builders to develop even further south, to create a nice area, with quality schools and so forth."

In fact, at the time, Disney owned a development company called Arvida. They had acquired it from Sid Bass and his brothers, Texas oil and real estate tycoons who, in Eisner's words, "had bought effective control of Disney during a takeover battle in 1984." Bass, as the majority stockholder, was also one of the major backstage players in naming Eisner to his position at

Magic Kingdom Park
Disney's Contemporary Resort
Discovery Island
BAY LAKE
Osprey Ridge Golf Course
SOUTH LAKE
LAKE MARBLE
North Service Area
Reams Road

Disney's Grand Floridian Resort & Spa
SEVEN SEAS LAGOON
Disney's River Country
Disney's Wilderness Lodge
Disney's Fort Wilderness Resort & Campground
Disney's Bonnet Creek Golf Club
Eagle Pines Golf Course

Magnolia Golf Course
Disney's Polynesian Resort
Shades of Green
Palm Golf Course
Walt Disney World Speedway
Car Care Center
Vista Blvd.
Proposed Vista Blvd.
Vista Blvd.
Disney's Dixie Landings Resort
Administration Area
Centra Care Walk-In Medical Clinic
RCID Planning & Engineering
Amateur Athletic Union
RCID Administration
Grosvenor Resort
Buena Vista Palace
Cross Roads Shopping Center

RCID Wastewater Treatment Facility
EPCOT Center Drive
Disney's Port Orleans Resort
Disney's Old Key West Resort
Disney's Saratoga Springs Resort
LITTLE LAKE BRYAN

Disney's Beach Club Resort
Disney's Yacht Club Resort
Walt Disney World Dolphin
Walt Disney World Swan
Fantasia Gardens & Fairways
Epcot
Community Drive
Lake Buena Vista Golf Club
Downtown Disney
Buena Vista Drive
Doubletree Guest Suite Resort
Royal Plaza
Courtyard Marriott
Vista Way Apartments
The Hilton
Sun Trust Bank
Casting Center

Tree Farm
Disney's Coronado Springs Resort
Western Beltway Connection
Disney's Animal Kingdom Theme Park
Disney's Blizzard Beach Water
Disney's Animal Kingdom Lodge
Buena Vista Drive
Exxon
Disney's Boardwalk Inn & Villas
Disney-MGM Studios
Osceola Pkwy
R.C.E.S. Headquarters
Disney's Typhoon Lagoon Water Park
Disney's Caribbean Beach Resort
Disney's Pop Century Resort
Exxon
Team Disney

Back-of-House DAK
Disney's All Star Music Resort
Disney's Wide World of Sports Complex
Osceola Pkwy
Osceola Parkway
Osceola
Orange

Magnolia Office Complex
Disney's All Star Sports Resort
Disney's All Star Movies Resort
US 192

Celebration Place
Celebration Golf Course
North Village
Celebration Village
Market Street
Lake Evalyn
West Village
South Village
Celebration
World Drive

S.R. 532

LEGEND
WDW BOUNDARY
EXISTING ROADS
PROPOSED ROADS
WALT DISNEY WORLD
CELEBRATION

Disney; the former president of Arvida, Chuck Cobb, was a member of the Disney board of directors. This was a power bloc that was not used to letting volatile real estate lay fallow.

Eisner, however, had no interest in "just another housing development," by which he meant the kind of suburban communities one sees all over the country, although it certainly would have been the easier and cheaper option. Eisner, taking a cue from Walt, perhaps, was looking forward, not back, not even back to Walt's imagined future, informed, as it was, by notions already decades out of date by 1984.

Eisner and Wells decided to tap into some serious gray matter: they convened a conference on the future and assembled a panel of leaders of industry and technology whose business was to know—or at least predict—the shape of things to come. The purpose of the think tank was to distill a picture of things yet to be, to assess what real-life needs were likely to be rising on the horizon, how those needs would and could be met, and how those vectors intersected with the business goals of the Disney corporation.

Among those present at that conclave were architect/planner Jaquelin T. Robertson, principal of Cooper, Robertson & Partners in New York City, a man of enormous intelligence and a firm grasp of the history of architecture (he is a former dean of the architecture school at the University of Virginia). According to Robertson, "The Disney people had proposed a look at the future of the Florida property that was, as I saw it, just awful. It was an elaborate rehashing of worn-out notions and discarded ideas—just some worked-over version of Walt's beehive plan—which is what I said when they asked for responses.

"I said that I thought it was nonsense and that I wouldn't consider doing any of it.... I thought that they should build a mixed-use residential community with all the best aspects of the best towns in America—

because this country has produced some of the best towns ever built anywhere. And that was the last I heard of it." At least for a while. Michael Graves, the only other independent architect at the conference, agreed with Robertson.

As it happens, Eisner's father, J. Lester Eisner, had been a developer. He served as the eastern regional head of the Housing and Urban Renewal Authority under Dwight D. Eisenhower ("before it became a cabinet post," Eisner remembers). He later became head of public housing for New York State under Governor Nelson A. Rockefeller. So by 1987, when Disney's own development division, headed by Peter Rummell, presented—among several serious alternatives for the Osceola property—a possible residential community, Eisner was intrigued if not fully convinced (other Disney decision-makers would take longer to persuade).

"The residential idea was met with considerable skepticism," remembers Peter Rummell. "The primary reason was that this isn't what Disney does. They were movie and theme park people."

"It's impossible to overstate the hostility that greeted the idea of a town among those in power," remembers architect Robert A.M. Stern, who is dean of the School of Architecture at Yale University. "There were people on the board," he remembers, "who thought it was the stupidest possible idea. Not only was it not what the company did, it was expensive. It would never earn the kind of money Disney expected of its investments, and it would expose the company in the arena of public opinion."

But the ground beneath the reluctant holdouts was beginning to swell from a vague proposal into a plan with curbs and drains and buried fiber optics. Walt's abandoned dream of a City of the Future, Eisner's own fascination with the possibility of build-ing a new neotraditional town, which increased over the coming decade, coincided not only with the

This map shows Celebration's location within Walt Disney's original land purchase.

growth of the New Urbanist movement in town planning, but also with an increasingly vocal and powerful environmental lobby. There were fears that the state of Florida could lay claim to Disney's ecosensitive Osceola County land—now worth many times the $200 an acre Walt paid for it—forbidding any kind of development whatever in perpetuity.

As the town idea began to take shape, one of its essential mandates, which came directly from Michael Eisner, was that it had to be something special. It had to be something no one else could or would do. It could not be "just another housing development"; it had to be Disney, in the best sense of the word. The new town would have to entertain and delight.

The landscape of the Florida property before the transformation: rugged and environmentally sensitive.

It would have to live up to the highest levels of expectation. But Disney had never before built a town, so just what did the Eisner dictum mean?

Right from the start of his tenure, the young CEO showed a keen personal interest in architecture, particularly as a way of ratcheting up Disney's corporate profile on a worldwide basis. In fact, at the end of their second week at Disney, Eisner and Wells held a now-mythic dinner for the company's design and development executives, a group that included architect/planner Wing Chao, a former student of Jaque Robertson's at Harvard.

"We had this dinner," recalls Chao (who is now executive vice president, master planning, architecture, and design, Walt Disney Imagineering), "and Michael proposed that we build a hotel in Burbank in the shape of Mickey Mouse. One foot would be on one side of Riverside Drive and one on the other. I remember that we all greeted the suggestion with silence. We didn't know if he was serious or joking."

"Years later," wrote Eisner in his autobiography, *Work in Progress: Risking Failure, Surviving Success,* "Wing Chao told me that it was as if 'a big bomb had been dropped in our laps.' My purpose was to stress the importance of theatricality and innovation. In my heart, I knew that a hotel shaped like Mickey ... probably was going too far.... Still, by pushing the envelope and suggesting the impossible, a lively debate was sparked. Several people at the table— most obviously Wing and Marty [Sklar]—left feeling enthusiastic about bringing more ambition to our design." Eisner immediately backed down from his Hotel Mickey idea when the pragmatic Wing Chao asked the simple question: "Where do we put the elevator?"

In a memo to Frank Wells in late 1985, Eisner set forth some of his aspirations for the company, aspirations that would play a major role in the evolution of Celebration. "If we're going to imprint our stamp on the world," Eisner wrote, "if we're going to do something more than help people have a good time with Mickey Mouse, if we're going to make aesthetic choices, then we've got to upgrade the level of our architecture and try to leave something behind for others."

So while his planners, developers, and Imagineers began exploring residential possibilities for the 10,000 acres south of U.S.192, Eisner was beginning to put his theories into practice. The first projects to come under his scrutiny were two huge resort hotels on Disney World property that would be designed by postmodernist master Michael Graves. The Princeton professor's Swan and Dolphin hotels opened near Epcot and the Disney-MGM Studios in 1989 and 1990, respectively, among much international ballyhoo and helped define Disney architecture in the Eisner years.

"We learned that good design didn't have to cost significantly more than bad design," explains Eisner, "that great architecture could be lighthearted, colorful, and metaphorical, in marked contrast to the cold, abstract modernist idiom.... The best design, like the best of any art, needs to be challenging and provocative, even a little threatening at first. At the same time, we tried never to take ourselves too seriously. As important as it was to design buildings that were aesthetically pleasing, they also had to be fun and entertaining."

"Before Eisner," remembers Peter Rummell, "the slogan of real estate development was 'location, location, location.' After Michael it became 'entertainment, entertainment, entertainment.'" And although he says it lightly, emphasizing humor, it's clear that the joke contains a significant truth.

And that's when "serious architecture" began to accommodate "serious entertainment" in a way that would prove to have extensive social and aesthetic ramifications. That's when familiar pop culture icons introduced by Disney began showing up as architectural leitmotifs. Disney's forays into architecture would revel in the characters the company had created in the course of seven decades of the twentieth century.

This process of moving "high temple" architecture into the circus tent, while not an entirely new idea (note the Coliseum in Rome), was certainly a notion generally abandoned by academic architecture after the Bauhaus, which thrived in the years between the two World Wars. It was, however, already part of the Disney aesthetic, if only implicitly.

It certainly informed the building of Disneyland in the early 1950s: "The buildings on Main Street are recognizable as archetypes but they aren't authentic," wrote Beth Dunlop in *The Art of Disney Architecture*. "They were drawn the way a town in a picture book or an animated film might be and then transformed into three-dimensional entities." This isn't just a central village street, despite serving a similar function and the meticulous replication of authentic detailing. Rather, it's the Main Street *attraction*, a reality passed through a filter of entertainment and bounced back to the collective imagination.

The architects of the Eisner era were getting a big kick (and making a big impact) by creating real, highly functional buildings that were enchanting and beautiful at the same time. Graves topped his Disney World hotels with enormous sculptures of swans and dolphins. Soon Eisner's architects, wrangled by Wing Chao, were finding inspiration for Disney buildings in the cartoon characters that Americans (and others) seemed to accept as inherent genetic material in the helix of popular culture.

Robert A.M. Stern's animation building at Burbank centered on a soaring wizard's hat of the kind Mickey wore as the Sorcerer's Apprentice in the original *Fantasia*. Michael Graves's office building on the same studio property featured seven enormous dwarves holding up the roof in the manner of the classical caryatids at the Acropolis in Athens. And when Robert Venturi and Denise Scott Brown came to design a building for Reedy Creek's fire department and ambulance crew, which serve Walt Disney World, they clothed it in black spots that invoke *101 Dalmatians*.

By the time Celebration was being shepherded through its conceptual design process in the late 1980s and early 1990s, Eisner and company had hired some of the best architects in the world—both established and emerging, market-tested and still edgy. They were commissioned to design cutting-edge buildings in Burbank and Orlando, as well as in Paris for the European version of Disneyland. In the process, they helped shape the course of modern architecture in the direction of playfulness and color, of childlike enthusiasm as a legitimate addition to time-tested academic/historical principles.

In all, during the 1980s and 1990s, the Disney company erected over one hundred signature buildings by such architects and firms as Robert A.M. Stern;

Gwathmey-Siegel; Venturi, Scott Brown and Associates; Aldo Rossi; Arata Isozaki; Arquitectonica; and Antoine Predock, among others, all of them major architects with the well-deserved respect of their profession. Disney and Eisner were beginning to win both recognition and praise for their serious patronage of architecture. And if the buildings do not endure as long as those like the Acropolis, built in Greece in the fifth century B.C., they are at least as identifiable in their own time.

Tracing the exact trajectory of Celebration from brainchild to thriving community is no easy task. For one thing, it was a complex process. For another, there is no one single version, since no one person is privy to all the steps, missteps, countersteps, and eventual strides in the staccato journey to fruition.

Even Michael Eisner admits that when he uses the first-person pronoun in recounting the history of Celebration, he acknowledges that he gave the go-ahead to the ideas of many individuals. And, as Stern says, "just who had what idea and in what order is probably impossible to remember, particularly since there were so many individuals and firms working on this project, and some people were bound to have had the same idea or reach a similar conclusion at the same time."

Essentially, however, the narrative through line goes like this: Until Michael Eisner, speaking for the Disney company, was fully persuaded to build Celebration, sometime in 1991, the course of planning did not run smoothly, or at least the route from conception to fabrication was not direct. Between 1984 and 1994 (that is, from the conference on the future to the groundbreaking of Celebration), the cumulative process that would result in the construction of a new town south of U.S.192 was circuitous—some might say torturous. It was an uphill trek full of bumps, delays, and detours: a battery of studies, competitions, submissions, design charettes, and refinements fed the hopper of possibilities.

"At one point," remembers Peter Rummell, "Celebration was going to be modeled on a factory town, like Hershey, Pennsylvania, which is a tourist destination where people pay to watch other people make chocolate."

Throughout the conceptual and design process the notion of creating an attraction to justify the town kept colliding with more normally residential notions: would anyone pay a gate fee to watch someone working in a shop? Ultimately, Rummell remembers, "No one could figure out what could be made or produced in our new town that would draw these tourists."

Another model for the new development was the college town. Celebration was to have been designed around a sprawling educational campus. In fact, disentangling the notion of a town from various amusement and/or personal improvement proposals was part of the zigzagging evolution of the place. Even after Celebration was inhabited, the relationship between the town and tourists to the Walt Disney World Resort had to be fine-tuned.

The first architectural competition for what would become Celebration was held in 1987. Four firms were invited to submit plans. They were Robert A.M. Stern

The Eisner era has been marked by unprecedented architectural energy. Michael Graves designed Walt Disney World's Swan and Dolphin hotels (THIS PAGE) and the Team Disney building at the Burbank studio (OPPOSITE).

Architects, which had already established close ties to Disney; Duany Plater-Zyberk, the firm behind the preeminent New Town resort community of Seaside, Florida; Gwathmey-Siegel, architects of the convention center at the Contemporary Resort and the Bonnett Creek Golf Course Clubhouse, both at Walt Disney World; and Edward Durrell Stone, Jr., the highly regarded landscape architect and son of an even more famous architect.

"The Stone plan," remembers Robertson, "was the one that was the most reality-based, which is to say, it followed all the conventional wisdom of real estate development and land use that were then popular. The rest of us were off in worlds that were anathema to the real estate guys."

Eisner did not find any of the four plans entirely successful on its own, although each had intriguing aspects he was interested in preserving. This tough-minded form of collaboration, the "one from column A, one from column B" modus operandi, as Stern describes it, became the norm for working on

Celebration. Eisner asked Stern, whose architecture was suffused with American arts-and-crafts influences (he designed the shingle-style Beach Club and Yacht Club resorts at Disney World), and Gwathmey-Siegel (known primarily for geometric Bauhaus-inspired white-concrete forms) to produce a collaborative plan. The plan was submitted and, as far as the architects knew, shelved while other projects—Disneyland Paris, for example—asserted claims on the resources of the Imagineers.

When the Celebration project was put back on the front burner, another design competition was held. For this round, Peter Rummell and Wing Chao added Charles Moore, Jaquelin T. Robertson, and Skidmore Owings Merrill, one of the largest architecture offices in the world (their many high-rise giga-buildings include both the Sears Tower and the John Hancock Center in Chicago and the proposed Freedom Tower at the site of the World Trade Center in New York). When SOM bowed out, the assignment of developing the master plan for Celebration fell fortuitously to Stern and Robertson working in tandem.

Stern and Robertson make an odd couple. Everything about Robertson, who is tall, loose limbed, almost folksy in his demeanor, suggests patrician lineage, right down to the twang of Harvard Yard in his voice. Stern, shorter, more compact, and alive with the bubbling energy of someone constantly between appointments, is the picture of a self-made man who takes nothing for granted. As it happens, the two work well together, theorist and realist roles shifting easily between them like good cop and bad cop. They share certain philosophies of architecture, have a mutual respect for one another, and are, in fact, friends.

As architects of the master plan for Celebration, Stern and Robertson began to turn out drawings and models, working in concert with Peter Rummell and his colleagues at Disney Development Corporation,

Concept drawings for a residential community on Disney's Osceola County property show the influence of early American town planning. These were created by Robert A.M. Stern Architects for the first architectural competition in 1987.

which at the time included Wing Chao. As the development program changed, so did the design, a process that was repeated many times.

"At first," remembers Stern, "the Disney Institute was at the center of Celebration, but it was removed and built elsewhere." The problem that sank the Celebration/Disney Institute marriage was parking. "We couldn't figure out how to build the roads or provide the parking in a small residential town for fifteen thousand people to attend a concert at night. I mean, the logistics were a nightmare, and who would want to live there? The great modernist design dictum," quips Stern, "is 'form follows function.' In town planning it's 'form follows parking.'"

What the architects, designers, planners, and Disney executives had decided by the end of the 1980s was that the way to the future was not a glass bubble with hovercraft zipping around invisible aerial roadways. Rather, it was a long look backward, to those traditional towns that American homeowners seemed to hunger for. Celebration would come to have, like Disney himself, one foot in the past and another in the future; it would be served by technology but not cowed by it. It would exist in the real world, but it would sample historical models.

"We looked back to Walt's future city and kind of jumped past him," recalls Wing Chao. "We realized that the future is not necessarily slick and faceless, with cold, unfriendly glass and steel buildings of no character. We did extensive sociological research as well as intensive studies of planned communities in America from its inception to the present."

As late as 1989, internal memos show, the Disney company's New Town bore many vestigial similarities to Walt Disney's original vision. It was imagined, for example, that there might be a train station on U.S. 192 and a bullet train that would carry passengers to nearby cities as well as the Orlando airport. But while some of the notions Peter Rummell included in his summary overview to Michael Eisner in 1989 were ultimately jettisoned, many others were eventually adopted in full.

"Much of the magic from the Magic Kingdom comes from the suspension of reality when you walk in the door," Rummell wrote to Eisner. "Our new Park will be exactly the opposite: It will not be controlled access or even gated in the traditional sense. Quite to the contrary, it will be the ultimate reality: a place where people actually live, work, shop, and play on a twenty-four-hour basis."

Rummell went on to describe "a wonderful residential town east of I-4 that has a human scale with sidewalks and bicycles and parks and the kind of architecture that is sophisticated and timeless. It will have fiber optics and smart houses, but the feel will, in many cases be closer to Main Street than to Future World. Nothing here different for the sake of being different, but designed to be enduring and comfortable.... We will focus on that which is wonderful and livable and will stand the test of time."

But this town would have a unique identity. It would derive, Rummell proposed, from three related principles: one, "the sophistication and detail of the urban design with its attention to the human scale in its landscape, pedestrian orientation, and streetscape"; two, "a careful attention to building design"; and, three, "an attitude about the future and a series of relationships that only Disney can produce that will underscore our commitment to this living laboratory." The key, Rummell concluded, was not in any one of these pieces of the pie but in the way they fit together to make "a place that really does work a little better and feel a little nicer and live a little easier."

Looking at all the evidence, Eisner took the leap. After all, as Walt himself said: "I've always had a feeling that any time you can experiment, you ought to do it. You'll never know what will come out of it."

Finally, in April of 1991, after seven years of ongoing conceptualization, The Walt Disney Company announced that it would create a town called Celebration essentially adjacent to The Walt Disney World Resort. The actual design of the community as a unique physical entity as well as a way of life would continue up to and beyond the arrival of the first residents in June of 1996. And that planning would directly affect the way the town looks and the way it functions—particularly with respect to the town's administration and with the Five Cornerstones that serve as the philosophical pillars of the community.

In the course of conceiving Celebration as a place with no exact precedents, and from the many market studies and focus groups the new Celebration Company held, it became clear that Celebration's target market was looking for some of the same values deemed critical by the planners at Disney Development.

Homeowners, concluded Todd Mansfield, then executive vice president of development, "will be looking for strong civic infrastructure. It will become our responsibility as community developers to establish it." The planning of Celebration, then, would be an exercise in community building as well as an experiment in land use.

"To build this civic infrastructure," Mansfield continued, "we'll have to form alliances with school districts, health-care providers, environmental organizations, communications companies, public

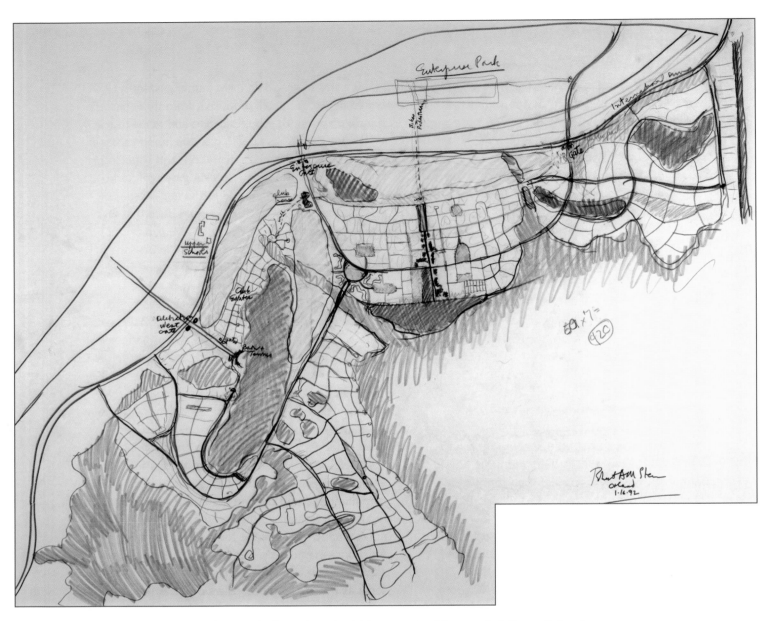

A late-stage land-use scheme for Celebration centered the property farther south than the
ultimate site, which was largely dictated by natural "islands" of land suitable for building.

agencies, and civic clubs as well. In 2010," he predicted,
"relationships and alliances like these will be as
important to the building of new communities as
hammers and nails."

From the philosophical predilections of the
planners as well as the perceived heartfelt desires of
home buyers, certain universal underpinnings were
beginning to emerge. These would become articulated
as the Five Cornerstones of Celebration, which would
inform the planning and construction of Celebration as
well as its future governance. Those Five Cornerstones
are Health, Education, Technology, Sense of
Community, and Sense of Place.

The Five Cornerstones, a set of concepts that act as beacons for Celebration, include a significant emphasis on health. The Celebration logo of a girl on her bicycle was designed by Pentagram.

HEALTH Celebration is perhaps singular in the attention it has paid to good health as a key to a good life and to the inclusion of health-driven concerns in the everyday life of the place. This cornerstone makes explicit what is evident in the community as it was being built, that the town as a whole wants to stay healthy in every meaning of the word. "Health" is a broad concept in Celebration; it includes both prevention and care and considers the whole person (body, mind, and spirit) in addition to the well-being of the community at large.

EDUCATION Securing a good education for their children is among the most important reasons residents report for moving into Celebration. It is part of a general desire to provide the best for their children that most parents naturally feel, and nowhere is education taken more seriously than in Celebration. The Disney company itself has made public education a high priority, working in numerous ways throughout the country in a host of programs and recognizing excellent teachers in an annual awards competition. From the beginning it was clear that schools in Celebration would have to be top-notch and that the town would have to provide a wide variety of educational experiences, both for children and adults, since Celebration is conceived as a fertile environment for lifelong learning.

TECHNOLOGY While Celebration would not be a City of the Future as imagined by Walt Disney, it would, nonetheless, make use of the latest available technologies, particularly in the arena of communication. The infrastructure exists for sophisticated electronic connections. A technology committee examines the ways in which new developments in science may be put into practice at the consumer level in Celebration.

SENSE OF COMMUNITY "More than anything else," runs one of the early Celebration promotional flyers, "what the residents of Celebration have in common is a shared vision for what life could be." Indeed, it is exactly the desire for a relationship with one's neighbors that drew most of the early residents to Celebration and continues to be one of the salient characteristics of the place. Community is the answer, at least in large part, to that sense people have of society as disoriented and isolating. And that pervasive malaise holds true in cities, where next-door neighbors may never see one another, and in suburbs, where neighbors sometimes see each other only from their cars.

"One of the last focus groups we did," Robert A.M. Stern remembers, "showed that there was an almost even split in the way people want to live. About 50 percent want to live in a tight-knit community and to interact with their neighbors; the other 50 percent want some version of living out in the woods by themselves." People from the second group do not flock to Celebration.

SENSE OF PLACE Just how would Celebration assert itself as a place different from all others? How would it look? What would be the defining characteristics? Of all the cornerstones, the notion of Place is perhaps the most elusive. Yet it informs the architecture, the ratio of residential to commercial building, the way traffic flows, and the layout of parks. This sense of Place is not abstract; it's palpable to anyone who turns off any of the main traffic arteries into Celebration, which exists, both physically and socially—even emotionally—as a specific entity.

"I always feel an enormous sense of relief whenever I see that white fence," says resident Paul Cooney referring to the white fence that separates the roadside greenery from Celebration Avenue at the approach to the town. "When I see that fence, I know I'm home. It's like my heart rate slows and even my breathing becomes more relaxed."

The road from inception to completion took the most creative thinking of the architects and planners, Disney executives, corporate partners, and elected and appointed government officials at local and state levels. It took convincing and compromising and required the input of scores of interested individuals and nonprofit community agencies to redact a workable plan from all the hopes, dreams, and possibilities for Celebration. But once committed, Eisner and the Disney company pushed forward for the best possible realization they could construct for their New Town. Celebration would strike, like the name itself, a note of optimism about America's future.

But first, of course, Celebration would have to be built.

Celebration ranks highest among American communities in nonpolluting electric vehicles per capita. The town's man-made lake, part of a complex water management scheme, is home to many native species. Architect Jaquelin T. Robertson designed the golf course clubhouse (OPPOSITE).

2. BUILDING

A TOWN

After eight years of meticulous planning—and addressing such complex issues as the precise location of the town and minimizing potentially negative environmental impact on the sensitive land—the Stern/Robertson master plan was complete. Having moved the heavens, not to mention some reluctant executive angels, it was now time to move the earth. The groundbreaking for Celebration took place in the spring of 1994. That same year, road paving and construction began. But just what were these backward-looking futurists going to build?

"One of America's great treasures is its extraordinary collection of traditional neighborhoods. All across this land, in large cities, small towns, villages, and rural hamlets you will find groups of houses built over the course of two hundred years with remarkable charm and character. Much though we admire the variety and individuality of these houses, we are most struck by the way in which each individual house relates to its neighbors and how they all serve to create a sense of community." —*Celebration Pattern Book*

Before they were able to reach any final decisions about their community, the Celebration team did what architects often do. They undertook a precedent study, researching the plans of some of America's greatest towns. Among the many models considered were such southeastern landmarks as Savannah, Charleston, Key West, and the old Garden District of New Orleans, as well as picturesque locations in New England and the mid-Atlantic and planned communities of the late twentieth century.

The planning team hired a young architect named Joseph Barnes, an intern in the firm of Charles Fraser (Peter Rummell's mentor and an adviser to the Celebration project), to photograph in architectural detail the kinds of successful towns that Celebration aspired to reinterpret for the twenty-first century. After analyzing the data, the planners made several core decisions.

First, they would settle on a date of the mid-1940s as the style cutoff date for the architecture of the town. Everything in Celebration would look as if it could have been built (at least in the imagination) before World War II and the subsequent upending of America's long town-planning tradition.

They also reduced all the possibilities to six styles that were typical of evolving village living, particularly in the Southeast. They were Classical, Colonial, French, Coastal, Mediterranean, and Victorian. These housing types, as Jaque Robertson explains, represent an American cross-pollination of the housing types of England, France, Holland, and Spain that characterized building in North America for some 150 to 200 years.

Each of these styles of home would be available in a variety of set price points on lots of predetermined size. For the first phase of development there were only four, in addition to apartments: Cottages, Village Homes, Estate Homes, and Townhouses (additional categories were added in the course of Celebration's build-out). Each of the housing types could be built in any of the six approved styles. The custom-designed Estate Homes were to be the largest and most expensive; the rest would be production houses, each with a limited number of variations in size and layout. Within limits set by the builders, certain custom options were possible for a price; and most parcels were sold with the option of adding an above-garage apartment.

The planners took another risk with the housing stock, opting for mingling the most expensive plots with the most affordable, cottages and town houses with veritable mansions. Given financial parameters from Disney, the planning team tried to imagine a town in which income and level of economic security were not the only defining traits of neighborhoods or even individual streets.

One of the ways they achieved this goal—and many others—was to create a system of service alleys between the backs of houses. This is where the garages would be situated, for example, and electricity meters; this is where garbage collection would happen and contractors' vehicles could park. The alleys, which were once a normal feature of efficient towns—and which work brilliantly, for example, in Beverly Hills— also create, says Robertson, an additional level of social discourse that speaks to the essential democratic impulse of Celebration.

"It's an invariable principle of real estate," says Robertson, "that expensive homes face expensive homes and so forth, so when we laid out the parcels we did that. But the alleys are a different story. You can back up a Village Home to a Cottage or to an Estate Home. And this is where people put out their trash and wash their cars, and you start to relate to this second set of neighbors, who aren't separated from you behind a landscaped back fence. We created, in effect, an additional arena for neighborliness that isn't tied to the value of the homes."

"I'm not saying that we solved all the problems of the world," says Stern of Celebration's intentional economic mix, "but we did create an environment that allows for much greater diversity, at least economic diversity, than any town that had ever been built before. That's one of Celebration's successes."

Major voices in the world of master-planned communities agree. Writing in *Urban Land,* the magazine of the Urban Land Institute (a professional advocacy group for responsible land use), Andrés

Duany, one of the acknowledged trailblazers and torch carriers for the New Urbanism movement, if not its unofficial guru, was exceedingly complimentary:

"Celebration remains one of the most intricate and accomplished examples of urban development since the 1930s. The diversity of housing built in close proximity at Celebration breaks new ground with its inclusion of rental apartments and row houses seamlessly integrated with single-family houses and mansions."

He goes on to praise Celebration for solving more planning problems than he managed himself at Seaside: "Celebration's plan...makes several important improvements to the new urbanist models, such as Seaside, Florida. For example, true alleys were provided

Celebration was conceived and designed as a reinterpretation of a traditional American town for a new century.

to accommodate the parking, whereas in Seaside the few planned alleys have been gentrified. In addition, the privacy of the backyards was carefully secured by the design of the units, while in Seaside, such outdoor privacy is neglected."

By placing the garages behind the homes, the architects of Celebration not only provided for parking that would not crowd the tree-lined residential streets ("form follows parking")—they relieved the builders of the Celebration homes of the difficulty of designing garages into the street facades. Where most housing

The town is designed to maximize contact between neighbors, whether it's in the service alleys between the blocks or the lovely parks around which many of the homes cluster.

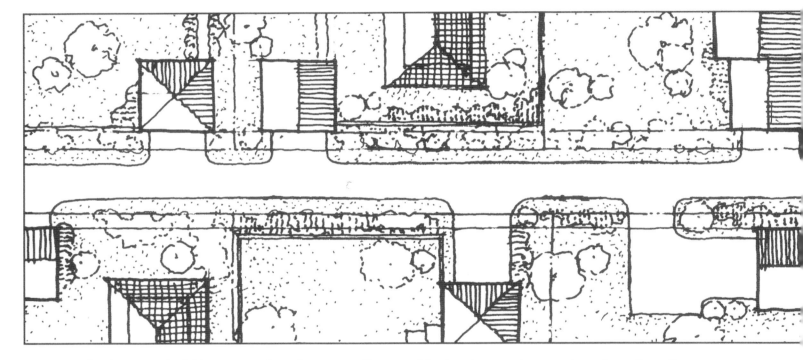

developments look like a procession of garages with houses attached, anyone ambling down the streets of Celebration would see porches, not garages. This not only underscored the town's commitment to walkability, it increased human contact.

"The garage," says Wing Chao, "is one of the most antisocial devices in architectural history. You enter the garage directly from your home, you get in the car, and if you even see a neighbor it may just be to wave as you both back down your driveways on the way to work."

There were many additional decisions made that shape the look of Celebration and give it a unique sense of place. No two adjacent houses, for example, may be identical, even among the production homes.

Varying dormers, bays, and porch configurations keep the town from looking like the carbon-copy suburban sprawls of the mid-twentieth century. Adjacent homes cannot be the same color, either, or face a home of the identical color (except white, which is universally permitted).

In addition to providing a certain diversity (Americans are justifiably proud of our "rugged individualism"), the planners wanted to create a uniformity that would help give the town its identity. It would further aid, overtly and subliminally, in the molding of the community. Front porches—one of Michael Eisner's required features from the earliest planning stages—are the norm in Celebration, and they exist for more than their architectural quaintness.

They are symbolic of openness and availability, and they are meant to be used.

No developer can force a family to use its porch, of course, but their very existence certainly offers an opportunity for social contact that was routine in the kinds of towns that inspired Celebration. The porches also serve as a mitigating zone in the progression from the street (the most public arena) to the sidewalk, the front yard, the porch (the most private of the public areas), and the privacy of the home itself.

As might be expected, the planners had very specific notions of height, mass, and setback: how big a house on a specific lot can be, how close it can be to its neighbor (or how far away), and how far from the street. All the decisions the planners made were contrived to maximize community rather than individual use. All the homes, for example, are close to the sidewalks and to each other; backyards are small.

The largest lots in Celebration, given to homes that range upward in value from $750,000, are around a third of an acre (90 feet wide by 130 feet deep). The smallest detached-home sites are just under 2,600 square feet. Critics of Disney in general, and the Celebration project particularly, claim that this density is a corporate ploy to dress avarice as social welfare. In fact, the mixed use of the land is not the most profitable path Disney could have taken.

"Variety and variance in real estate is expensive," instructs Peter Rummell, "and the old Levittown houses were exactly the same and very cheap. People will pay for taste and design, but it is always a tough judgment as to where you stop tweaking. Celebration could have been done more cheaply—but it wouldn't be the place it is."

By limiting backyard space, however, and keeping houses closer together and nearer the tree-lined streets, the Celebration alchemists were attempting to turn the lead of American suburban development into the pure gold of community-mindedness. Families at Celebration would have their own homes—they would not have to share kitchen facilities with their neighbors, for example, in the way of the evolving cohousing movement—but to maximize their options for recreation, for example, Celebration's citizens were going to have to venture out into the public spaces.

Another significant decision that had to be made was just who would be brokering sales in the new town.

The Celebration Company, as developer, was originally allied with another Disney subsidiary, Celebration Realty (which has since turned sales over to the individual builders). The only task Disney would not take on itself (and it was considered) was actually building the homes, apartments, and town houses.

Estate Homes would be custom-built by half a dozen highly regarded Orlando-area firms. Responsibility for the production homes was ultimately assigned to David Weekley Homes, a Houston-based builder who gained some experience in Central Florida while the Celebration plan percolated through its planning process. Townhouses would be built by Town & Country, a reputable firm based in Chicago with a good track record for customer satisfaction, research showed, but no Florida experience.

To make sure these diverse builders (and others yet to come) were all on the same page with respect to the overarching design philosophy of Celebration, the planners once again moved forward by looking back. They would create an official *Celebration Pattern Book,* in essence a book of instructions to builders that codifies the design principles, from volume to detailing. This innocent-looking, relatively unassuming paperback publication (hardly bigger than

an ambitious college paper) would go a long way to giving Celebration its own sense of place. And while the covenants that govern the town allow for significant individual expression, the planners wanted to establish a set of codes that would, simultaneously, give the town its desired cohesiveness.

Pattern books are not new. Jaque Robertson notes that they've been around since the Romans. They were certainly in widespread use in the expanding United States of the eighteenth and nineteenth centuries. Sourcebooks of sound architectural ideas and the latest decorative flourishes, they are the reason why so many of the homes in the thousands of small towns across America look so much alike. They were as unifying in their way as the Sears & Roebuck catalog once was and as television is today. These pattern books were essential tools for local builders in the days before architects were available to every middle-class consumer. Pattern books fell into disuse after World War II when home construction had to be fast and cheap with aesthetic choices kept to a minimum.

"In the past," reads the *Celebration Pattern Book,* "there was a consensus among builders, architects, planners, developers, and home buyers on the form and style of good neighborhoods and houses. The

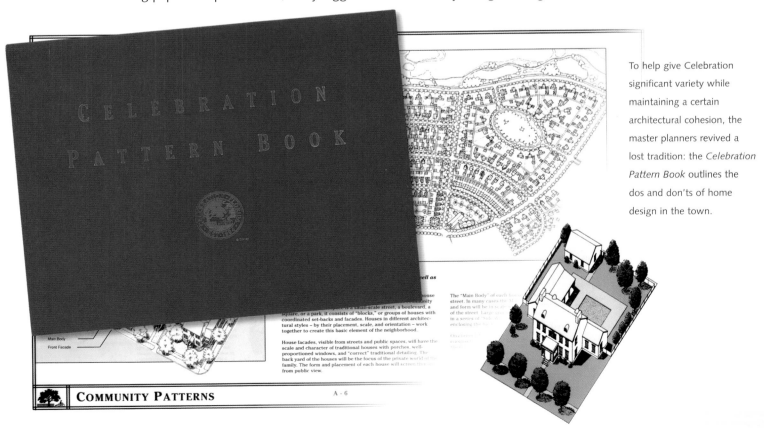

To help give Celebration significant variety while maintaining a certain architectural cohesion, the master planners revived a lost tradition: the *Celebration Pattern Book* outlines the dos and don'ts of home design in the town.

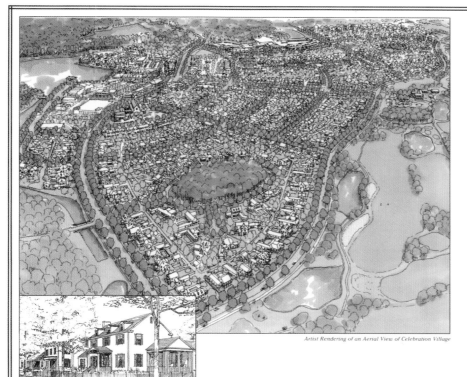

The town of Celebration is being built in the great tradition of American community building.

Conceived as a small Southern town, Celebration is being developed with an understanding of the community design methods used to create some of America's best neighborhoods and towns. Rather than reconstructing the past, Celebration will carry forward the best town-making traditions into the twenty-first century.

A series of residential neighborhoods, each centered around a significant public space, are intended to be built over time. Comfortable tree-lined streets, squares, and parks are envisioned which will provide the setting for houses, townhouses and apartments. The character of the community spaces will vary from neighborhood to neighborhood, but they will be defined, to a large extent, by the personality of the houses that face them.

While each house will provide comfortable private areas in its back yard, it also will be oriented to the street with a front facade that welcomes neighbors. Each house will offer at least one "gift" to the street; for example, a large columned porch, a classical portal for the front door, a loggia, or a special architectural element such as a bay window, portico or balcony. The community spaces, therefore, will be created through a close collaboration between neighborhood houses and landscaping.

The houses will be designed and built by many different builders and individuals. In order to create community space, the design of each house will be required to respond to the individual character of the street, park, or square which it faces. This calls for a coordinated approach to designing houses, in which front facades and all parts visible from public spaces are in harmony with each other and with Celebration's goal of building a community.

In the past, there was a consensus among builders, architects, planners, developers, and home buyers on the form and style of good neighborhoods and houses. The design principles that represented this consensus were contained in *Pattern Books* which were used by builders to create neighborhoods and towns. The details and overall principles for designing houses were set out clearly in these Pattern Books, which were illustrated with a combination of three-dimensional images of the desired result and details of key elements such as porches or windows.

Pattern Books gradually disappeared after the Second World War and the consensus among architects, developers, builders, and the general public has deteriorated. In order to restore that consensus, the design guidelines for Celebration have been prepared as a Pattern Book, a revival of this great American tradition. In order to prepare the Pattern Book, we studied Pattern Books from the 18th and 19th Centuries, visited and analyzed a number of small towns in the Southeastern United States, and applied the lessons learned to current development practices. As an introduction to the Pattern Book, we include a summary of these studies on the following pages.

Artist Rendering of an Aerial View of Celebration Village

design principles that represented this consensus were contained in Pattern Books, which were used by builders to create neighborhoods and towns. The details and overall principles for designing houses were set out clearly in these Pattern Books, which were illustrated with a combination of three-dimensional images of the desired result and details of key elements such as porches or windows. . . .

"In order to restore that consensus, the design guidelines for Celebration have been prepared as a Pattern Book, a revival of this great American tradition. In order to prepare the *Pattern Book*, we studied pattern books from the eighteenth and nineteenth centuries, visited and analyzed a number of small towns in the Southeastern United States, and applied the lessons learned to current development practices."

Trends and Innovations in Master-Planned Communities, a book published by the Urban Land Institute in 1998, enumerates the communities: "As part of its research in 1992, approximately fifteen members of the Disney team took a weeklong tour of older towns and newly built communities, visiting Columbia, Kentlands, and Avenel in Maryland;

Charleston, Kiawah, Hilton Head, and Sea Pines in South Carolina; Savannah, Georgia; and Boca Raton's Mizner Park, Coral Gables, and Seaside in Florida. Charles Fraser, developer of Sea Pines and a special consultant to Disney throughout the planning for Celebration, coordinated the tour and is credited with coalescing the team's perspective. Jim Rouse, developer of Columbia, inspired the team to think of the community as a 'garden to grow people in' and to understand that a successful community needs to have a strong and compelling vision."

The *Celebration Pattern Book* as it now exists is, essentially, a blueprint for creating acceptable blueprints, including ground plans, elevations, surfacing materials, decoration, landscaping, roofing, and fences. Such major issues as mass, setback, and siting are clearly delineated for each of the six main housing types (Classical, Victorian, Colonial Revival, Coastal, Mediterranean, and French) approved by the planners. The parameters for the six housing types were established in consultation with six individual architectural firms across the United States, each of them known for their work in historical forms.

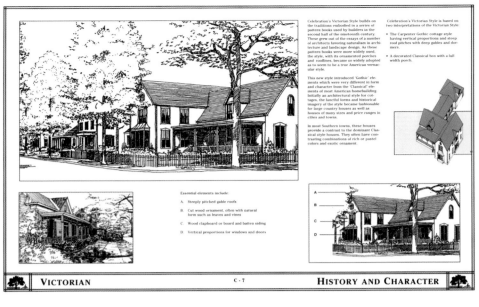

Celebration's Victorian Style builds on the traditions embodied in a series of pattern books used by builders in the second half of the nineteenth century. These grew out of the essays of a number of architects favoring naturalism in architecture and landscape design. As these pattern books were more widely used, the style, with its ornamented porches and rooflines, became so widely adopted as to seem to be a true American vernacular style.

This new style introduced 'Gothic' elements which were very different in form and character from the 'Classical' elements of most American homebuilding. Initially as architectural style for cottages, the fanciful forms and historical imagery of the style became fashionable for large country houses as well as houses of many sizes and price ranges in cities and towns.

In most Southern towns, these houses provide a contrast to the dominant Classical style houses. They often have contrasting combinations of rich or pastel colors and exotic ornament.

Celebration's Victorian Style is based on two interpretations of the Victorian Style:

- The Carpenter Gothic cottage style having vertical proportions and steep roof pitches with deep gables and dormers.
- A decorated Classical box with a full width porch.

Essential elements include:

A. Steeply pitched gable roofs

B. Cut wood ornament, often with natural form such as leaves and vines

C. Wood clapboard or board and batten siding

D. Vertical proportions for windows and doors

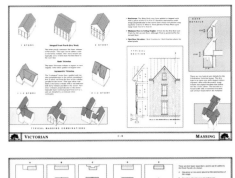

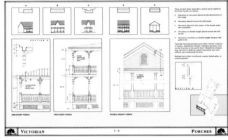

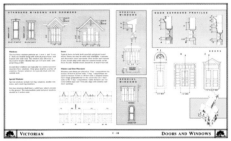

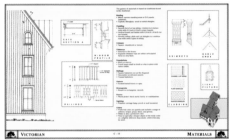

Six styles of home in half a dozen sizes with significant leeway in decoration make for more architectural diversity than most planned communities and allow homeowners to express themselves aesthetically.

24'

32'

36'

40'

24'

32'

36'

40'

28'

32'

36'

40'

28'

32'

This page illustrates a range of possibilities for house designs using the Celebration Victorian pattern. The possibilities are grouped by typical widths of the Main Body of the house.

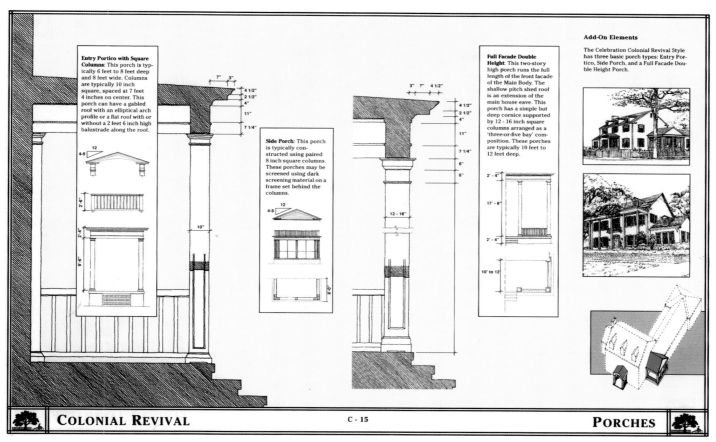

Entry Portico with Square Columns: This porch is typically 6 feet to 8 feet deep and 8 feet wide. Columns are typically 10 inch square, spaced at 7 feet 4 inches on center. This porch can have a gabled roof with an elliptical arch profile or a flat roof with or without a 2 feet 6 inch high balustrade along the roof.

Side Porch: This porch is typically constructed using paired 8 inch square columns. These porches may be screened using dark screening material on a frame set behind the columns.

Full Facade Double Height: This two-story high porch runs the full length of the front facade of the Main Body. The shallow pitch shed roof is an extension of the main house eave. This porch has a simple but deep cornice supported by 12 - 16 inch square columns arranged as a 'three-or-five bay' composition. These porches are typically 10 feet to 12 feet deep.

Add-On Elements

The Celebration Colonial Revival Style has three basic porch types: Entry Portico, Side Porch, and a Full Facade Double Height Porch.

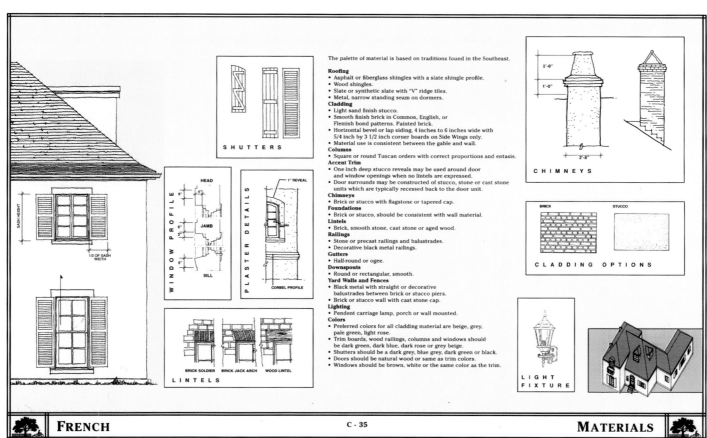

SHUTTERS

WINDOW PROFILE

HEAD

JAMB

SILL

PLASTER DETAILS

1" REVEAL

CORBEL PROFILE

BRICK SOLDIER   BRICK JACK ARCH   WOOD LINTEL

LINTELS

The palette of material is based on traditions found in the Southeast.

Roofing
- Asphalt or fiberglass shingles with a slate shingle profile.
- Wood shingles.
- Slate or synthetic slate with "V" ridge tiles.
- Metal, narrow standing seam on dormers.

Cladding
- Light sand finish stucco.
- Smooth finish brick in Common, English, or Flemish bond patterns. Painted brick.
- Horizontal bevel or lap siding, 4 inches to 6 inches wide with 5/4 inch by 3 1/2 inch corner boards on Side Wings only.
- Material use is consistent between the gable and wall.

Columns
- Square or round Tuscan orders with correct proportions and entasis.

Accent Trim
- One inch deep stucco reveals may be used around door and window openings when no lintels are expressed.
- Door surrounds may be constructed of stucco, stone or cast stone units which are typically recessed back to the door unit.

Chimneys
- Brick or stucco with flagstone or tapered cap.

Foundations
- Brick or stucco, should be consistent with wall material.

Lintels
- Brick, smooth stone, cast stone or aged wood.

Railings
- Stone or precast railings and balustrades.
- Decorative black metal railings.

Gutters
- Half-round or ogee.

Downspouts
- Round or rectangular, smooth.

Yard Walls and Fences
- Black metal with straight or decorative balustrades between brick or stucco piers.
- Brick or stucco wall with cast stone cap.

Lighting
- Pendent carriage lamp, porch or wall mounted.

Colors
- Preferred colors for all cladding material are beige, grey, pale green, light rose.
- Trim boards, wood railings, columns and windows should be dark green, dark blue, dark rose or grey beige.
- Shutters should be a dark grey, blue grey, dark green or black.
- Doors should be natural wood or same as trim colors.
- Windows should be brown, white or the same color as the trim.

CHIMNEYS

BRICK   STUCCO

CLADDING OPTIONS

LIGHT FIXTURE

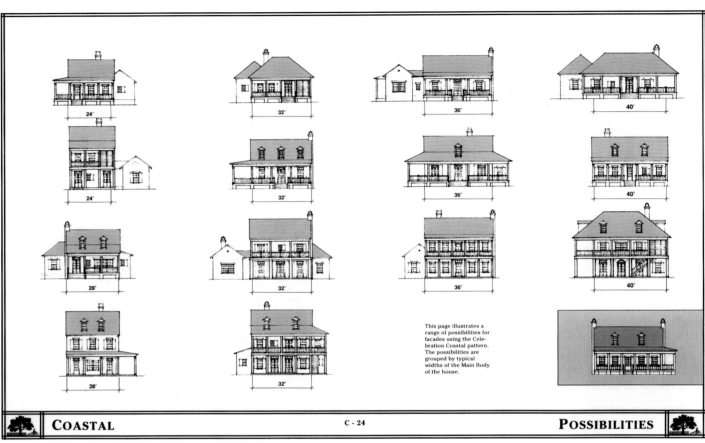

This page illustrates a range of possibilities for facades using the Celebration Coastal pattern. The possibilities are grouped by typical widths of the Main Body of the house.

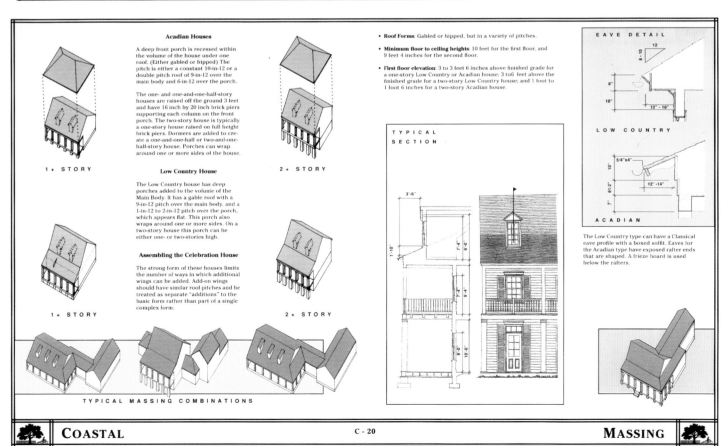

Acadian Houses

A deep front porch is recessed within the volume of the house under one roof. (Either gabled or hipped) The pitch is either a constant 10-in-12 or a double pitch roof of 9-in-12 over the main body and 6-in-12 over the porch.

The one- and one-and-one-half-story houses are raised off the ground 3 feet and have 16 inch by 20 inch brick piers supporting each column on the front porch. The two-story house is typically a one-story house raised on full height brick piers. Dormers are added to create a one-and-one-half or two-and-one-half-story house. Porches can wrap around one or more sides of the house.

1 + STORY   2 + STORY

Low Country House

The Low Country house has deep porches added to the volume of the Main Body. It has a gable roof with a 9-in-12 pitch over the main body, and a 1-in-12 to 2-in-12 pitch over the porch, which appears flat. This porch also wraps around one or more sides. On a two-story house this porch can be either one- or two-stories high.

Assembling the Celebration House

The strong form of these houses limits the number of ways in which additional wings can be added. Add-on wings should have similar roof pitches and be treated as separate "additions" to the basic form rather than part of a single complex form.

1 + STORY   2 + STORY

TYPICAL MASSING COMBINATIONS

- **Roof Forms**: Gabled or hipped, but in a variety of pitches.

- **Minimum floor to ceiling heights**: 10 feet for the first floor, and 9 feet 4 inches for the second floor.

- **First floor elevation**: 3 to 3 feet 6 inches above finished grade for a one-story Low Country or Acadian house; 3 to 6 feet above the finished grade for a two-story Low Country house; and 1 foot to 1 foot 6 inches for a two-story Acadian house.

TYPICAL SECTION

EAVE DETAIL

LOW COUNTRY

ACADIAN

The Low Country type can have a Classical eave profile with a boxed soffit. Eaves for the Acadian type have exposed rafter ends that are shaped. A frieze board is used below the rafters.

In a bold and uncommon move, Celebration's town planners developed the community's town center before buidling its homes. A group of Celebration's planners, architects, landscapers, and designers posed for a photo at the end of Market Street for the opening of the Town Center. Seated (FROM LEFT) are Peter Rummell, Robert A.M. Stern, Michael Eisner, and Jaquelin T. Robertson.

The *Celebration Pattern Book,* coordinated by Ray Gindroz of Urban Design Associates (UDA) in Pittsburgh, says Andrés Duany, "has a precision, clarity and completeness that should elicit admiration from anyone who studies it as an intellectual achievement."

In order to establish the visual vocabulary of Celebration, Robert A.M. Stern and Jaquelin T. Robertson themselves would design the so-called "background" buildings, the sixteen two- and three-story structures in "downtown" Celebration, an area known as Market Street after its major shopping avenue. These buildings would hold the retail stores, restaurants, apartments, services, businesses, and other organizations that would serve Celebration. The bulk of parking for this mixed retail/dining/residential district would be behind the buildings, in lots formed by the rectilinear building blocks. (There is also nonmetered street parking throughout Celebration.)

Just which of the two master planners would design what building was a matter easily dispatched by the collaborators. "It took about ten minutes to

decide," Robert Stern recalls. "I think we sketched it out on a napkin. We said, 'Here, you do this and I'll do this....' We did decide that we would not design any two adjacent buildings, in order to make sure there was some variety of viewpoint and sensibility."

"I am most impressed by...the 'background buildings'—the ordinary buildings that give character to a town," wrote architect and eminent social historian Witold Rybczynski in the *New Yorker* in 1996. "[T]hey manage to be both unpretentious and charming, which is more difficult to achieve than it sounds."

The master planners left space alongside and interspersed with this pastel environment for certain architectural "jewels." The idea was that the new, modern buildings would look as if they had been added to the town years after the background buildings. Parcels of land were especially set apart for these public-use buildings, serving the purpose of what might be called a Civic Center. To design these "iconic buildings," Disney turned to its wish list of great architects, many of whom had already worked for Disney.

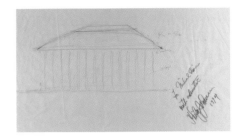

TOWN HALL
PHILIP JOHNSON

Philip Johnson, a leading modernist for decades (he's now in his nineties), was asked to design the Town Hall at one of the corners of Market Street and Celebration Avenue. Johnson came to fame in the 1950s for, among other things, his absolutely stripped-down glass houses, houses with sheer "glass curtains" in lieu of exterior walls. In the 1980s, Johnson had designed a skyscraper for AT&T in Manhattan that was topped by a giant neoclassical pediment (the kind homes might have had in the America of George Washington and Thomas Jefferson). It, too, was among the most talked-about buildings of its day—albeit a controversial one (it is now owned by Sony).

"When we asked him to design the Town Hall," remembers Robert Stern, "he said something like, 'I don't do classicism anymore.' So we said, 'Well, Philip, it's only been about ten years—maybe you could try to remember how you used to do it.'"

Johnson's Town Hall for Celebration is a two-story, colonial-inspired redbrick building that blends small-town tradition and a modernist line. It plays with proportion, especially with the pillars that hold up the overhanging roof. These columns—there are fifty-two of them—are much thinner and more closely spaced than the Greek-revival buildings of the eighteenth and nineteenth centuries, but there is no mistaking the function of the building. This is clearly the place were the administration of the town is conducted. It houses the office of Town Hall's executive director, Pat Wasson (who is sometimes referred to as the "Town Manager") as well as the conference room where most of the town's committee meetings are held, including meetings of the Celebration Residential Owners Association (CROA).

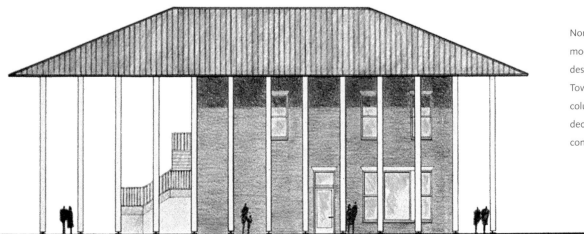

Nonagenarian American modernist Philip Johnson designed Celebration's Town Hall with traditional columns but with minimal decoration and a serious contemporary twist.

Beside Town Hall would be the post office, a bona fide branch of the United States Postal System (the nearest branch is about ten miles away, off U.S. 192 in Kissimmee). The Celebration post office is so necessary that it's busy all the time.

The post office, with its echoes of Tuscany and a stand of exterior mailboxes (another of the town's points of interaction), was designed by postmodernist Michael Graves (architect of the Swan and Dolphin hotels).

As Michael Eisner tells it, he gave Graves the smallest iconic building in Celebration because the hotels were the biggest on any Disney property. In any case, the cylindrical tower that holds the entry doors of the post office makes an appealing curved counterpoint to the marching verticals of Johnson's adjacent Town Hall. The smooth geometry of the post office, which uses tinted stucco and arresting fenestration as its primary decoration, contrasts and complements its other neighbor, too—a pale yellow traditional "background" building that houses retail shops and apartments.

Set into the semicircular entry to Market Street is a small landscaped park called Market Square. It has an old-time tiered fountain and views up Water Street to the golf course clubhouse and down Market Street to the lake. It also has traditional park benches where anyone can enjoy a salad or sandwich from Goodings, the town's grocery/market/convenience store.

POST OFFICE

MICHAEL GRAVES

The outdoor mailboxes at the post office designed by Michael Graves are another example of providing congenial occasions for contact between neighbors.

Opposite the Town Hall, across Market Square, is another signature building, this one created by the late Charles Moore of Moore Andersson Architects, a gentleman almost revered by his peers. As things happened, it would prove to be his last design. Originally conceived as the town's Preview Center, the building has a redbrick tower wrapped in a white wooden staircase. Quite purposefully, it's the highest point in Town Center.

Moore's attractive building hearkens back to the wildcat days of Florida development when these "storm lookout" towers were built as markers on the flat horizon announcing new real estate opportunities. It has a nearby precedent, too: the tower built by George Merrick, founder of Coral Gables, Florida. The Preview Center is now being turned over to retail space: Bank of America opened on the ground floor in 2003 as Celebration's second bank.

PREVIEW CENTER
CHARLES MOORE

The late Charles Moore designed the highest structure in the Town Center. Such towers are familiar landmarks in the southeastern U.S.

An incredibly photogenic piece of work, the cinema looks good at virtually any time of day, particularly from the walking path at the far side of the lake, and especially at sunset.

CESAR PELLI

Intersecting Market Street along Town Center Lake is Front Street, another block of commercial/residential buildings, this one featuring the town's excellent eateries: Celebration Town Tavern, Market Street Café, Café D'Antonio, Seito Japanese Restaurant, and Columbia Restaurant. Front Street is the entertainment center of Celebration, and its signature building is a twin-towered movie theater designed in the retro-Hollywood Art Deco style by former Yale Architecture dean, Cesar Pelli.

Among the inspirations for the twin-screen AMC theater was the Cathay Circle cinema in Los Angeles, where *Snow White and the Seven Dwarfs* premiered in 1937. Handily adjacent to the movie house is Herman's Ice Cream Shoppe, the town's ice cream and sandwich shop. Pelli designed another notable building with two "spires": the Petronas Towers in Kuala Lumpur, the tallest structures on earth pending the erection of the Freedom Tower at the site of the World Trade Center in New York City.

Across the street from the movie theater is a fountain that is a favorite recreational spot for children and parents alike. It's much like the ones at Epcot, at the Music Center in Los Angeles, and at Olympic Park in Atlanta; they spurt jets of water at seemingly random intervals, making it impossible to predict where the water will come from next. As hot as it sometimes gets in Central Florida, it's a conveniently cooling form of fun and a favorite of Celebration's kids.

This fountain is part of the Celebration waterfront promenade, which extends to a meandering nature walk around Town Center Lake. Where Front Street meets the foot of Market Street, a concrete "patio" steps down to the water. There are a dozen or more old-fashioned rocking chairs here (some under umbrellas), and they're not chained in place. Instead, they're available for sitting in whatever configuration you and your friends might like. It serves as a meeting and resting place and on weekend nights hops with teenage life. (It's also where the local firefighters park when they come into town for lunch—most of Celebration's parking is behind and between the commercial buildings.)

Visitors to town sometimes chuckle at the sign that rises out of the water at the bottom of the lowest step of the patio. The sign states that it is illegal to annoy or feed alligators. This is not a joke. The lake is indeed home to at least one adolescent reptile (the local fauna is carefully monitored and will be relocated if it becomes a significant danger to the human or canine population). Alligators are a fact of life in Central Florida and, in most cases, hikers and crocodilians give each other a wide enough berth.

The Celebration Hotel (OPPOSITE) rises above Town Center Lake, which forms a focal point for community activities as well as a comfortable place for some leisurely conversation.

BANK OF CELEBRATION

ROBERT VENTURI
& DENISE SCOTT BROWN

Among the other iconic buildings commissioned for the opening of Celebration was the Celebration School, designed by Boston architect William Rawn. The Bank of Celebration building (currently occupied by SunTrust Bank), designed by the husband-and-wife team of Robert Venturi and Denise Scott Brown, intentionally omits a drive-through, an isolating innovation that allows patrons to do their banking without interacting with one another.

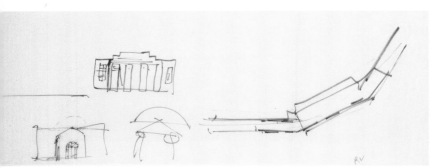

In this highly walkable Town Center, office buildings, the bank, and the school are all just moments away. Celebration Place, a short distance from Town Center, is home to medical facilities and several more office buidlings.

But in the fall of 1995, all of this idyllic architecture was just a construction zone barely higher than the horizon. None of the houses had been built, or even designed. There were no model homes, there were no models of homes. There weren't even any drawings. But that's when lots went on sale, in a series of tents erected in an empty field in the commercial zone that is now called Celebration Place.

Anticipating an interest exceeding the housing units becoming available in Phase One—and wanting to be scrupulously fair—The Celebration Company decided to sell the first 351 houses and rent the first 123 apartments with an "anyone can enter" old-fashioned drawing.

On November 18, 1995—now recognized in town as Founders' Day—some five thousand people showed up to participate in the drawing. They put down 1,200 refundable deposits of $1,000 each. Prospective homeowners were permitted to join two of the individual lotteries for each of the four housing types. Also part of the local lore is that people remember their lottery numbers, which is still a topic of conversation among original residents.

On June 18, 1996, Larry and Terri Haber and their children, Brandon and Staci (pictured opposite), moved into the home they bought after the Founders' Day drawing seven months before and became, for all time, the first residents of Celebration.

"We were pretty realistic. We knew Disney would do a great job, but we never thought it would be perfect. We thought it would be a good place for the kids to grow up." —*Larry and Terri Haber*

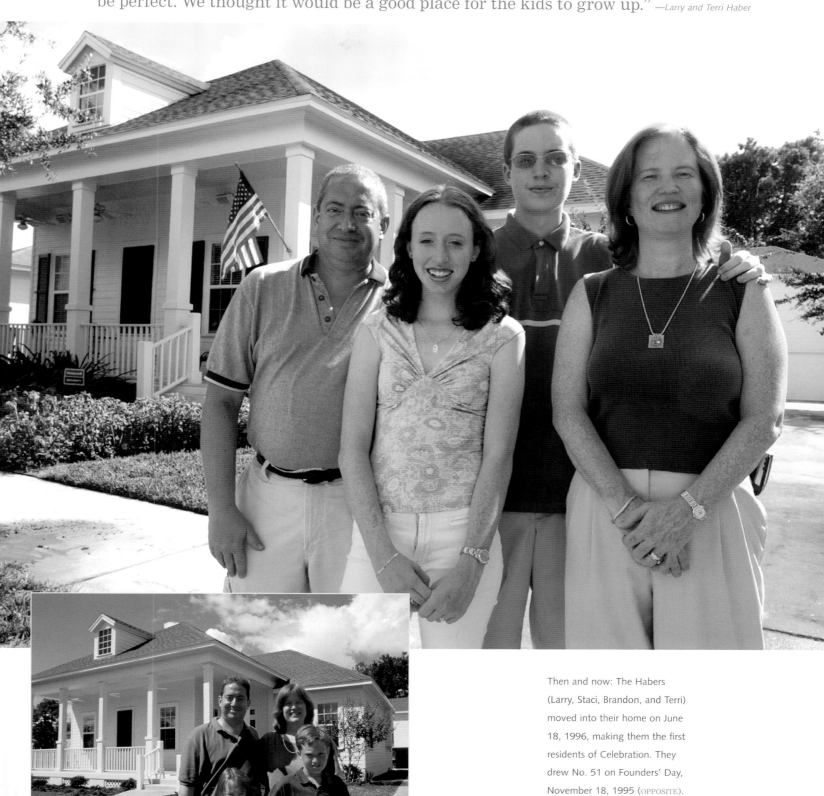

Then and now: The Habers (Larry, Staci, Brandon, and Terri) moved into their home on June 18, 1996, making them the first residents of Celebration. They drew No. 51 on Founders' Day, November 18, 1995 (OPPOSITE).

As homes started to go up, residents started to move in and arrange their furniture. Many of the promised amenities of Celebration were still "to come," but most of the pioneers ("I've been here since before Goodings," the real old-timers say) took it on faith that they would soon be completed. Journalists invited to meet the architects at the official opening of downtown Celebration in November 1996 were treated to a formal dinner inside a tent erected on the property of what is now the Celebration Hotel.

The 115-room hotel that opened in 1999 was artfully designed by Graham Gund Architects of Cambridge, Massachusetts, to recall a wood-framed hotel of Florida in the 1920s. It has shutters, awnings, and dormers, tin roofs with deep, low eaves, a brick entry courtyard, and a decorative lighthouse tower. It

also has an excellent restaurant, the Plantation Room, which is known locally for its updated Southern cuisine and Sunday brunches.

The hotel is one of Richard C. Kessler's Grand Theme Hotels, a small group of stylish, upscale hostelries that are rich in history. The hotel, which has some 5,000 square feet of meeting space, hosts numerous corporate seminars as well as weddings and special town events. The regular happy hour of the Celebrators (the town's organization for those over fifty) takes over the open lobby bar one Friday night each month, kicking up a lively ruckus with the help of the hotel's resident pianist.

The hotel, a member of the prestigious Preferred Hotels of the World network, is the summer residence of the NFL's Tampa Bay Buccaneers, whose summer

training camp is conducted at Disney's nearby Wide World of Sports Complex (winter home of the Atlanta Braves). The hotel has even named a suite in honor of Buccaneers head coach Jon Gruden; it faces the lake on one side and the pool area's hot tub on the other.

The 1996–97 school year was not conducted in the Celebration K–12 building because it wasn't ready until the following academic year. Fortunately, only 260 children enrolled in all the grades together (about 20 per year). The community's new children spent the educational part of their days in the Teaching Academy, another downtown William Rawn building, which was itself conceived as part of the community's overall educational plan.

Florida Hospital Celebration Health broke ground in November 1995, but the sprawling facility (it will reach 750,000 square feet by full build-out) did not open until 1997 (the inpatient units opened in 1998). Justifiably one of Celebration's pride and joys, the enormous complex is an impressive presence on the perimeter of the town. Taking a cue from the underlying philosophy of the administration and the Celebration town plan that health is an all-inclusive concept and that a hospital facility should be an inviting amenity to the well in addition to those in need of care, the complex was designed by Robert A.M. Stern in the manner of a grand spa hotel.

The soaring entry atrium of the Health Center is more like the hotel lobby of one of Disney's own large resort hotels—the Wilderness Lodge, for example—than a typical hospital. There is a registration desk and a lobby shop and numerous comfortable places to wait. It's bright and open and conveys a sense of normalcy and calm. Celebration Health also includes a 60,000-square-foot, state-of-the-art fitness center—the best in the region—that includes a large lap pool. It's a for-fee gym that draws on Celebration, Osceola, and Orange counties for its membership. There's even an excellent cafeteria, Seasons, which is open to the public and serves three meals a day plus midnight snacks. (The Celebration branch of the Rotary Club meets here for its weekly Friday 7 a.m. breakfast meeting.)

Celebration Health is run by Florida Hospital, the oldest and largest private hospital in the state. It is routinely named as one of the best hospitals in the country, recognized for such specialties as Heart

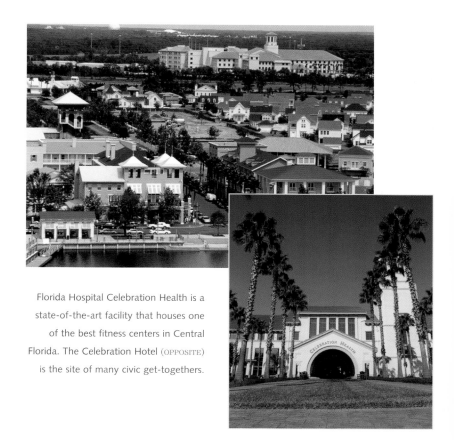

Florida Hospital Celebration Health is a state-of-the-art facility that houses one of the best fitness centers in Central Florida. The Celebration Hotel (OPPOSITE) is the site of many civic get-togethers.

Surgery; Neurology and Neurosurgery; Urology/Prostate Cancer; Hormonal Disorders (Diabetes); Digestive Disorders; and Kidney Disease.

Interestingly, although it is nondenominational in all its medical ministrations, the hospital is owned by the Seventh-Day Adventist Church. The eight million-member Christian denomination has been deeply involved in health care since the days of its founders, who early in the establishment of the health-related church sponsored the medical education of five young people (two of them women, highly unusual in the 1860s). One of the young male students was John Harvey Kellogg, whose family name is synonymous with cornflakes.

Adventists take "a sound mind in a sound body" even further, as a matter of faith. They believe, broadly speaking, that a healthy body is required to fully flourish spiritually. Most Adventists are vegetarians who abstain from all addictive substances, although the Celebration Health cafeteria offers many decidedly non-Adventist choices, meat and coffee included.

Thanks in part to technology alliances with medical-service providers, Celebration Health offers leading-edge procedures in many areas of medicine and is actively involved in advanced research. The facility provides the community with the kind of care envisioned in

Celebration's Health cornerstone. In order to customize its care to the Celebration community, Florida Hospital spent three years in consultation with an international who's who of health-care professionals, including former U.S. Surgeon General Dr. C. Everett Koop. Also adding advice, encouragement, and expertise in emerging technologies were representatives of Harvard University's Mind and Body Institute, Stanford's Center for Disease Prevention, the International Health Futures Network, and the National Institutes of Health.

Des Cummings, executive vice president of marketing for the Florida division of the nationwide

afloat. It's boring and people hate it. But at Celebration Health, it was found that playing the harmonica provides the same therapeutic benefits. Celebration now has an active, energetic forty-member harmonica band, which gives concerts and tours other hospital facilities.

Another point in the philosophy of Celebration Health involves keeping people out of hospitals and out of nursing homes in particular. As life expectancy increases, many people who are ill spend their last years in declining health in expensive, depressing facilities. Quality of life, even for the ill, is central to health here.

Karen Galanti availed herself of yoga for expectant mothers at Celebration Health right up to the week she delivered daughter Ella Pearl Galanti in the company of her family.

Adventist care system, spent most of five years in the process of developing the programs of Celebration Health and its physical plant. The hospital, he instructs, in keeping with Celebration's cornerstone philosophy, was to transform the notion of hospital from court of last resort to first line of defense.

"I call it the Listerine principle," says the affable Cummings, who moved his family to Celebration to be closer to the new building. "When you meet people in most towns, they say they're glad there's a good hospital nearby and they hope they never have to use it. It's like the old Listerine tag line: the taste you hate twice a day."

Celebration would try to make health both attractive and fun by integrating it with the whole life experience. Cummings relates the example of respiratory patients, those with life-threatening breathing diseases. The common treatment involves forcefully blowing into a tube to keep a Ping-Pong ball

One pulmonary patient, Cummings remembers, was a former diver for Jacques Cousteau. Unfortunately, the lifelong cigarette smoker destroyed his lungs. Not only could he not dive, but he had terminal emphysema. He was given three months to live. He lasted three years, without hospitalization, making appearances with the harmonica band.

Even the physical plant says "health," as it is understood and practiced by the Adventists. "You enter this facility over water," notes Cummings, adding that "God and Disney moved the lake." The water, he says, "sends a cue about the power of the natural environment to relieve stress. This is a system for the whole person as well as for entire lives."

As of 2004, Florida Hospital Celebration Health is a 400,000-square-foot facility of 120 beds (all in private rooms). It may in time nearly double in size (to 240 beds) and, in fact, Stern designed the building so that it could be replicated in mirror image at what is now the back of the center. The octagonal atrium will remain intact, in any expansion plan, and the main entrance remain stable in the life of the community.

The proactive health plan here says that a hospital is not just a place to go when you are sick. Rather, health is a lifelong process that can actually be enjoyable. In addition to its beds and state-of-the-art surgical and diagnostic facilities, there's a kids' gym with age-specific children's programming. There are aerobics studios and courts for basketball and volleyball in addition to weight/strength-training areas, the pool, and sauna and steam rooms for relaxing. Various 12-step programs hold meetings here; there's a dental clinic and yoga classes for expectant mothers. This is the place to come for an appointment with a nutritionist who will help devise an individual dietary plan or weight-loss program.

Ongoing events on the Celebration Health monthly calendar include the Alzheimer's Support Group, a Breast Feeding Friendship Network Luncheon, and Water Tai Chi. Occasional seminars cover topics from minimally invasive knee- and hip-replacement surgery, flu shots, and cooking (how to analyze recipes and substitute healthier ingredients). The Health Center also conducts several important annual invents, including a 5K and 10K walk/run that emphasizes the importance of exercise in a healthy lifestyle. Like Celebration itself, Celebration Health is an incredibly upbeat place.

Before any of the building in Celebration could take place, however, the planners had to decide where to put it. The siting of the town on the 10,000-acre Osceola County parcel proved to be a bit tricky given the region's aqueous topography and some very real environmental concerns shared by Disney and its neighbors in Florida.

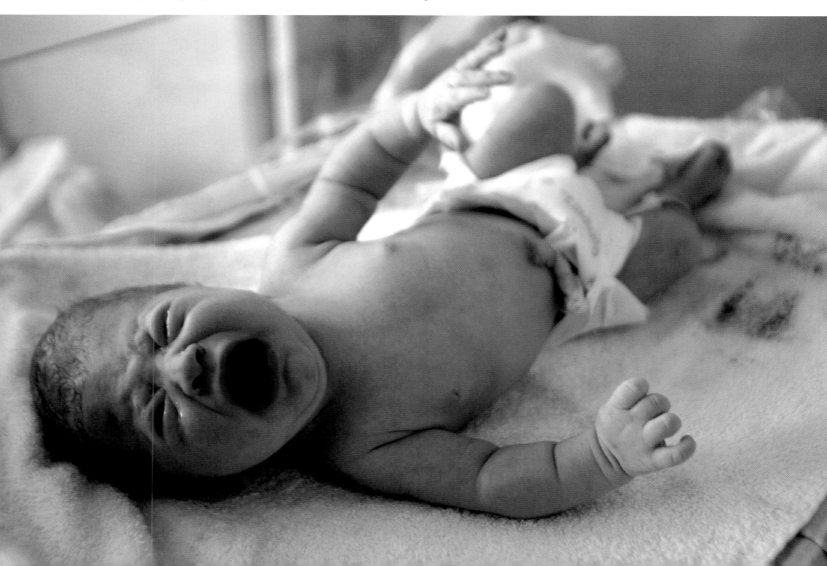

Celebration Place—the first buildings of which were designed by the late Aldo Rossi—
is the anchor of Celebration's outer-circle commercial community.

"The property is an archipelago," says Jaquelin T. Robertson. "It has islands of land you can build on that are set in the middle of what is, essentially, an ocean. So the location of the town was largely dictated by the lay of the land, literally. It just made the most sense to follow what is basically a shoreline." Still, the planners considered all the possible permutations of using the patchwork of dry land and marsh before the final decisions were made: in at least one extensive, near-final plan, the map of the town was skewed much farther west than in the final blueprint.

Man-made factors helped shape the siting of the town, too, notably the highway complex of Interstate 4, U.S. 192, and Florida's 417. Since the property was effectively split in two by "Road World" or "Highway World," as Robertson alternately calls it, it made more sense to embrace that reality instead of fighting it.

Stern and Robertson, working with Disney Development and EDAW, the internationally acclaimed landscape architecture firm, eventually settled a plan in which the entire community of Celebration would sit on 4,900 acres of extant, restored, and augmented

land. This would be surrounded by 4,700 undeveloped acres that would form a permanent greenbelt around the town (it's a nesting sanctuary for, among other avian species, the American Bald Eagle).

The southern boundary of the town would follow this greenbelt, its "natural shoreline." The northern and western outer belt of the town would consist of commercial and public-use property, including some 60 acres for the campus of Celebration Health. Here, too, is the 109-acre office park called Celebration Place.

When completed, Celebration Place (the layout of which resembles the Renaissance center of Pisa in Italy) will hold approximately ten buildings of one million combined square feet. The first buildings for Celebration Place were designed by the Pritzker Prize–winning architect Aldo Rossi (now deceased). Along with the hospital and Celebration Place, an additional stretch of outlying road will house some two million square feet of office, light industrial, and hotel space, creating a local employment hub that is not specifically related to the tourist industry.

Between the residential town and the outer industrial/greenbelt, is the par-72, public championship golf course. Designed by the father-and-son team of Robert Trent Jones, Sr. and Jr., it cradles the residential areas of town inside the arc of its manicured fairways. The downtown shopping and entertainment area is nestled, like a pearl in an oyster, at the center of the plan. Front Street runs alongside the 17-acre, man-made Town Center Lake, the town's focal point. The lake, which is surrounded by a popular walking/bike path that follows the natural lay of the land, also marks the soft boundary between the town and the undeveloped wetlands.

This overall scheme consists of concentric bands of use—fanning outward from the town center to the first tract of homes, then to the golf course and the non-retail business district beyond. The long, rolling swathes are intersected by a short, straight axis that runs from Town Center Lake to the 16,500-square-foot, pale yellow golf course clubhouse designed by Jaquelin T. Robertson in a style he calls Southern Carpenter Gothic. Its signature architectural feature is the kind of windmill you'd expect to see in earlier decades.

The town's layout, Robertson says, gives the map of central Celebration the look of an "uneven butterfly," with the short axis representing the body of the creature and the housing, public, and commercial precincts its wings. That main axis consists of two parts. The first, Market Street, is the main shopping street. The second leg of the axis, Water Street, is a wide residential avenue (almost an allée) with a narrow watercourse running between its north- and southbound lanes, forming a landscaped mall 138 feet wide. Two small auto/pedestrian bridges span the canal for east-west traffic.

The treatment of the golf course boundary was something of a forward-looking throwback. Thinking beyond cost per square foot to the life of the whole town, the planners insisted that the golf course, while it could face a street of million-dollar homes, should not be obstructed from public view. The scene as one drives alongside the fairways should not be of the backs of private residences, but, as Celebration was eventually built, with facades of unique custom-designed homes on one side of a meandering road that is absolutely open across the street. The golf course, therefore, became a visual as well as a recreational amenity, serving at least one of the functions of a public park: to create open space that allows a community to "breathe" in its landscape.

This use of the golf course as a buffer, with houses facing the fairways across a residential road, is one of the historical precedents revived for Celebration. "From 1900 to, say, 1930," instructs Robertson, "it was the normal thing to have a street of big houses on a road that overlooks the golf course. And that gives the town a very nice pastoral feel."

This notion of access, of public space, was extremely important to the Celebration planners. Many decisions about the way the town would be

The open green space of the Celebration Golf Course, a public course with no gates or fences, serves many of the functions of a park.

built were carefully chosen to communicate openness and welcome rather than exclusion and separation. There are deliberately no gates at the entrances to Celebration because the planners did not want the approach to the town to say "Keep Out," remarks Robert A.M. Stern.

Additionally, Celebration Avenue, the main road into Celebration, does not skirt the town but runs right through it, bridging the more residential areas and the retail downtown area with its associated public buildings and recreational facilities. While everyone in the environs of Celebration may not feel it, the underlying reality of the place is that all are indeed welcome to live, visit, shop, and dine in Celebration and to participate in its many cultural and community events.

For similar reasons it was decided that the Celebration School would be a public school and that it would not be placed on the periphery of town ("traditionally in the part of town where land is cheapest," says Stern). Instead, the K–12 (kindergarten through twelfth grade) school would be, as appropriate

to Celebration's education cornerstone, on a 35-acre campus right at the heart of town, just as schools were years ago. Children in Celebration are to be seen and heard, by design. Pedestrian paths were indicated in the plan between the town houses that face the school across Campus Street to make the daily commute to and from school as direct and safe as possible for kids on foot or any number of wheels (bicycles, scooters, in-line skates).

Siting issues were further compounded by the earnest desire of both the ecologically-concerned Disney company and outside conservationists to preserve wherever possible the area's native bio-systems.

"The Osceola County land was sensitive," Stern points out, "but it was not exactly virgin forest." Much of it had already been turned into farm and ranch land. The tract does, however, extend to the headlands of the Everglades, which is part of a water filtration/purification system that is critical to the health not only of Florida but of the globe. The Everglades is an abused and neglected system that's

The Celebration School, designed by William Rawn, is in the heart of the downtown area,
which helps integrate the children of town into the community at large.

finally in the process of being protected and repaired. Conservationists and government officials were justifiably concerned about the impact of large-scale residential development on, among, or adjacent to the wetlands, particularly since a Disney town would likely serve as a seed for greater growth in the area.

Generally speaking, in order to obtain the entitlements necessary for building on sensitive property, developers agree to maintain small plots of natural habitat in and among new homes. But Disney's planners wanted to go further. Instead of simply agreeing to maintain certain isolated stands of old growth, Disney bought an expansive parcel of wetlands and uplands (the former Walker Ranch) south of its already extensive holdings in Osceola County. Working with several public agencies and nonprofit environmental organizations, the company established the 8,500-acre Disney Wilderness Preserve (thanks largely to the shepherding efforts of Celebration's first general manager, Don Killoren).

Owned and managed by The Nature Conservancy, but substantially supported by Disney, the preserve, about 15 miles south of Walt Disney World, offers a trio of trails totaling seven miles through an otherwise undisturbed environment. There are numerous archaeological sites on the property, too, including a Seminole settlement dating to around A.D. 500. Disney is currently working with The Nature Conservancy to preserve and restore a complex of ecosystems that embraces pine flatwoods, scrub, palmetto prairie, freshwater marshes, and forested wetlands—home to many species of listed and endangered animals.

With Disney's help, The Nature Conservancy is performing restoration and management efforts—including the removal by staff and volunteers of invasive and nonnative plants. And the preserve's Environmental Education Center is a resource for Central Florida environmental leaders, as well as field experts, researchers, and conservationists. (The Disney Wilderness Preserve also helped to allay fears among some old-family Osceolans that Central Florida's authentic landscape would be entirely obliterated by development.)

But creating the Disney Wilderness Preserve did not mean that Celebration would strip its building sites, either. From the earliest stages, the master planners wanted to root the town of Celebration in its habitat. This was, of course, one of the core lessons of the career of Frank Lloyd Wright, who taught that a house on a hill should be "of" the hill, not merely "on" it.

Celebration was conceived to be entirely surrounded by nature, with stretches of conservation land intermingling with the homes, parks, and even the school. To get to the gymnasium of the Celebration School, for example, students must take a raised wooden pathway above preserved wetlands. This not only protects the environment; it provides a daily real-life lesson in ecology to the town's junior citizens.

Numerous parks would also serve the various neighborhoods of Celebration, and each park would be designed with a unified scheme that was appropriate to the size and style of the homes that face it. These parks and isolated wetlands help to tie the local flora and fauna to the built environment.

Preservationists were concerned, too, with mature trees on the Celebration property since development invariably involves cutting down big trees that are growing where roads have to be built. But the planners and builders made a pledge to keep as many of the old trees as possible and to plant numerous new trees to replace any that had to be eliminated for logistical reasons. Celebration's tree-saving program included moving as many trees as possible out of harm's way. Using the world's largest mechanical "spade" (it can scoop out a seven-ton crater), many of the healthy ancient oak trees were moved during construction to a holding area and were replanted, some of them in their original position, when it was safe.

As is common practice in the United States, the builders even recycled some of the earth itself. Much of the earth used to shore up the town against possible flooding came from the dig that created Town Center Lake. That lake was designed and constructed to be part of the town's drainage system; it can receive runoff from the canal along Water Street.

High on the long list of innovations in the development of Celebration was building the downtown before the homes were up, in a gesture familiar to fans of the film *Field of Dreams*: "If we build it, they will come." The decision was, in Michael Eisner's particularly accurate word, "counterintuitive." Historically, town centers arise from the needs of growing communities, not vice versa.

For Robert A.M. Stern, the creation of the town center in advance of the town's homes is one of the most important subplots in the complex Celebration story. "People are routinely promised downtown development by builders," Stern says, "but if it isn't there when people move in, their shopping patterns and restaurant patterns and whatever else are already set. They've gone elsewhere. If the downtown ever happens, it fails."

The downtown of Celebration would also be a mixed-use neighborhood with some of its 123 one- and two-bedroom apartments (700 to 1,200 square feet) built over street-level shops and restaurants. While not the most original idea in the world, this was fairly avant-garde for Central Florida in the 1990s.

"When we started," remembers Stern, "we were told that nobody would live on the south side of Orlando. Saying the words 'town house' and 'apartment house' in the Orlando real estate community was like saying 'bubonic plague.'" In fact, the town houses and apartments of Celebration are almost invariably fully occupied, with demand increasing so significantly that the company added more town houses and apartments than had been originally considered in the Celebration housing mix.

Bringing the population into the Town Center is part of the overall integration policy that informs every aspect of life in Celebration. People living downtown create an energy that encourages greater use. The apartments at ground level in many of the buildings were designed to convert to business spaces should the need arise. In fact, over time, numerous small businesses—among them real estate offices, a beauty salon, a framing shop, a doctor's office, and a dry cleaner—have opened in units that formerly served as residences.

Now you see it: the heart of downtown Celebration in model form
(OPPOSITE) and under construction in 1995–96 (ABOVE).

As the town continued expanding, in its physical plant as well as its population, Celebration entered a new beginning. The architecture, the social plan, and the flesh-and-blood population began to meet. The community of Celebration was about to be born, and it was not always an easy birth. The merging of individuals into a community, a coherent unit that makes room for personal expression, is probably the more inspiring aspect in the Celebration story. Planning and building the town would prove to be merely the exposition to the Celebration story. And as all students of narrative structure learn in school, what follows exposition is conflict.

OSCEOLA COUNTY FIRE STATION

3. CREATING A

SCHOOL ZONE

STOP

COMMUNITY

A brand-new town has the smell of fresh sawdust, new grass, and drying paint. It is rich in hope and ripe with anticipation, and Celebration was no exception. It was, as early as the summer of 1996, when the first families moved into town and started to lay carpet and unpack boxes of carefully packed belongings, flushed with the excitement of expectation. Everything had a first-time feel about it, and there was a lot to explore as more homes went up on just-paved streets.

What a new town does not have is history or tradition or a set of time-tested, locally preferred methods of getting things done. It has no mechanism for social interaction. It has no collective memory of crises survived—floods, famines, droughts. This can be a frightening or exhilarating situation, and, unsurprisingly, various freshman members of the Celebration community faced the unknown with some combination of both.

"The purpose of towns is not commerce, not manufacturing. The purpose of towns is living."

—Jaquelin T. Robertson

The homes of Celebration were built on "islands" of what Jaquelin Robertson refers to as an atoll in an ocean of preserved wetlands.

As it happened, the infant Celebration community did not have to wait long for its first test. The marsh soil was about to hit the swamp skimmer for the first time.

Unfortunately, construction of Celebration's homes, apartments, condominiums, and town houses coincided with a building boom—not only nationally and in the state of Florida, but in the environs of Orlando specifically. This caused a shortage of labor, and particularly a shortage of skilled subcontractors. David Weekley Homes had worked in the area and had established a network of reliable contacts. Town & Country, however, which was charged with constructing the town homes, had not.

Disney had promoted Celebration enthusiastically, not having foreseen the demand for homes that met the commencement of sales in 1995. David Weekley had not predicted the number of customizations its ruggedly individualist clients were negotiating for their production homes. And no one had guessed how many of the new residents would exercise the option to have an above-garage apartment built for parents, children, or guests.

Additionally, the homes in Celebration were not being built the way most of the homes in Florida have been built. The standards were higher, for example, and there was a great deal more decorative detail than the subcontractors were used to. The homes in Celebration are also built from a large number of high-tech, non-wood building products (wood rot and termites are major problems in high-humidity regions like Central Florida), and the crews were not used to working with them.

The building schedule began to lag, then to fall far behind. Residents who had been expecting to move into Celebration in July were now facing delays of weeks, then months, then as much as a year or more. Suddenly, the dream was becoming a hardship, with long commutes and family separations and temporary billeting with relatives all causing the kind of stress that buyers had not expected, certainly not of Disney. After all, there was no disquieting messiness at Disney World.

With the start of new home construction in 1995, Celebration's neighborhoods began to take shape.

As the contractors worked feverishly to meet their commitments, some mistakes were made in the earliest buildings, most of them minimal but some quite serious. The worst problems seemed to be with the town houses, which were (and are) highly sought after, despite assurances to The Celebration Company by local real estate pundits that no one would live in a town house south of Orlando.

It soon became clear that the demand for labor exceeded the supply of skilled workers. The more people the builders had to hire to speed delivery, the less experienced the crews were. In some cases, trim work got sloppy and ducts were crossed, columns began to tilt inward, promised alterations to standard schemes failed to materialize. Most egregiously, perhaps, in at least one block of town houses, the roofs leaked—significantly.

Naturally enough, thought the new residents, Disney would take care of the problems—although, as a rule in almost all communities, the contract for homes was between the homeowners and the builders, not the developer. And it is to the builders that homeowners should have applied for redress of grievances. Nonetheless, The Celebration Company did step in to pressure the builders to make good on their move-in dates and to improve the quality of their construction if it came into question.

But the scene was set for a real-life awakening on the part of some of the homeowners as well as the company. Disney was being held to its promises, some of which were authentic, some only imagined. The homeowners had expectations of their developer that sometimes far exceeded any reasonable standard. Unfortunately for Disney, it was the company's reputation for exceeding even extraordinary expectations that made the dissatisfied new residents feel perfectly justified in increasing their demands.

Some frustrated homeowners became angry. Celebration's executives were beginning to be seen as defensive rather than responsive. Celebration (a.k.a. "Disney") and the residents of the town were like a couple that has no mechanism to resolve conflict, and both, perhaps, were a bit stung by the construction problem. Ultimately, The Celebration Company was able to persuade the various builders to rectify construction defects, including replacing the roofs on the entire block of problem town houses, a make-good that is virtually unprecedented in development history.

Most of the new town residents were satisfied by Disney's efforts that the company was acting in good faith, but a minority were not. Some felt that the first difficulty between the developer and the buyers resulted in an *us vs. them* mentality that affected every future difference between the residents and The Celebration Company. It became clear to Disney that what they had offered as a creative and exciting new alternative living experience had been received by some as the promise of a Shangri-la, free from the problems of real life.

As houses were finished, families moved in. When completed, Celebration will be home to approximately twelve to fifteen thousand people.

If the building problem recharted the course of the Celebration Ship of State, the next problem had the potential to sink it. This concerned the Celebration School, which is a public school, and the tempest raised by a variety of parental issues with the school—some real, some overstated, some pure fiction—left casualties in its wake. If families could tread water while their homes were delayed and delayed again, they drew the line when it came to the education of their children.

Historically, Florida ranks nearly last among states in the amount of money spent per student on education and consequently the schools fare poorly. Many of Celebration's potential homeowners were prepared to leave good school systems only on the promise of something better. It was a promise eagerly extended by Disney, which had spent years trying to develop the best possible school for the town.

Following Michael Eisner's edict that a thing worth doing was worth doing better than anyone else could do it, the framers of the town's education system solicited the advice of the best education professionals they could find. With help from Disney, the Osceola County School Board turned to colleges and universities. Some were local, such as the University of Central Florida and Stetson University, Florida's oldest private college (whose main campus is in

DeLand, about 50 miles north of Celebration). Others were farther afield—Auburn in Georgia, for example, Johns Hopkins in Baltimore, and Harvard in Cambridge, Massachusetts. In all, representatives from seven institutions of higher learning came together to turn the best principles of education into a plan for schooling the children of Celebration.

These "best principles"—many of them tested and proven in schools across the nation—included what seemed to some to be relatively radical notions. Children in the Celebration K–12 would not be grouped by class, it was decided. Rather, a series of neighborhoods would be occupied by children of different ages. There would not be one teacher per classroom, but several—say, four teachers for as many as one hundred students, and they weren't to be called "teachers," either; they were "learning leaders." Teaching would be tailored to individual students, playing

Disney worked with officials from Osceola County and experts from seven prestigious universities to establish the education program of the Celebration School, which attempted to put into place the "best principles" of American public education.

to their individual strengths: visual, mathematical, conceptual, etc. New media replaced some books; there were no grades in the usual sense and there was little homework. Instead of dividing the school day into hours of math, science, and social studies, groups of students would design interdisciplinary "personal learning plans" that would range across several disciplines to solve a single problem or examine a single, but complex topic.

Many who moved to Celebration were anticipating the highly touted excellent schooling to be a return to reading, writing, and arithmetic. And many of the new families loved the idea that all their children would attend the same school together. Instead, they were getting a new-fangled school and a nomenclature many of them had a hard time grasping. If there were no tests and no grades, parents wanted to know, how could they tell if

A public county facility, the Celebration School is built on land donated by Disney and has received enhancement funds from The Celebration Company. Various civic organizations also raise money for the school, which was originally designed as a K–12 (Celebration High School opened in 2003).

their kids were learning? And how would the older kids have their interdisciplinary, multimedia projects evaluated when it came time to apply for college? How could the kindergartners possibly share space with their brothers and sisters in third and fourth and fifth grade?

If ever there were a case of multiple interpretations of the same event, it was the experience parents were having with the Celebration School, a terrific William Rawn building that stands proudly at the epicenter of the town. If there was a single truth, it was certainly not to be found in the charges and countercharges that were flying among the residents and between the residents and The Celebration Company.

Many families loved the school; others panicked, and for two solid years the conflicts bounced back and forth, with increasingly acrimonious pro-school and anti-school camps emerging. As in every community, most of the residents were more comfortable with a quieter, more centrist position. Extremists on both sides of the issue brought Celebration close to uncivil war. Some demanded the school to rein in its "kookiness"; others remained faithful

Although the school was the center of early controversy and tension between homeowners and The Celebration Company, in recent years it has consistently been given an A rating by the state of Florida.

to the most experimental possible solution. For some, "the school problem" was making schooling all but impossible.

The planners of the school, from the developers to the education experts, now acknowledge that the experiment they undertook so enthusiastically and so optimistically was too ambitious. While all those "best principles" that underlie the theory of education at Celebration are sound and work well in school districts around the country, no single school district had ever tried to use all the principles simultaneously.

Ultimately, the school curriculum was altered. Books, tests, and a grading system that parents could better understand were put in place. Children would still meet in neighborhoods, but the age range was reduced so that kids were in school with peers, not with those developmentally far behind or ahead. Not everyone was mollified, but attending classes became more a matter of going to school than of going into a battle zone.

The turmoil over the school did create some turnover in town. Many of the people who moved away were from the first wave of buyers. "They were the most idealistic," says Perry Reader, president of The Celebration Company from 1998 until 2004, "the most moved by the dream of

Disney Magic. Some of them weren't prepared to deal with a wing of Disney as a developer."

"We have people who have purchased houses who think they're moving to Utopia," noted Disney Development executive Todd Mansfield in the early years. "We keep having to remind them that we can't provide safeguards for all the ills of society. We will have everything that happens in any community."

Indeed, it became clear that some Celebration residents expected Disney to "take care of" failing marriages and unruly children as well as trash collection and mosquito control. They thought their lives would be a day in the theme park, literally, and they tended to be outspoken in their disillusionment. Many complained routinely to Reader and his colleagues at The Celebration Company; some actually took to writing directly to Michael Eisner with their problems.

Among the pioneers, however, were quite a few families who were able to make the adjustment to real life, and, of course, some never thought their home lives in Celebration would be as perfect as the artful milieu. And those who stayed through the building crisis and the school crisis began to come together in the way that towns do after a natural disaster: they found themselves stronger and, in some cases, more closely knit to their fellow travelers. Some residents today speak of the building snafu and the school controversy with a smile, a sigh, or a knowing roll of the eyes as an experience mutually survived.

Meanwhile, under the energetic direction of Dr. Susan Brasfield, a colorful and involved town resident as well as an outstanding educator, the Celebration School has now been named an A-level school (the highest category). Its students routinely perform well above average on the Florida Comprehensive Assessment Tests (FCATs), which attempt to quantify student performance in five areas. In 2003, the school scored 93 percent in writing, opposed to a state average of 81 percent. Gratifyingly, schools elsewhere in Osceola County are beginning to adopt some of the "best principles" of education that were first tested in Celebration.

Celebration residents tend to be a hands-on lot. Covenants apply to the outside of homes only; interiors are entirely up to the homeowners. AT RIGHT: Celebration School's director, Susan Brasfield, surveys her domain while speaking on her mobile phone.

Perry Reader, former president of The Celebration Company, oversaw the transition of the town from a plan to a functioning community of individuals. Family life is central to the Celebration experience.

Perry Reader credits the school's ultimate success to involved parents. Longtime PTSA member Susan Bona, whose family owns the Celebration Town Tavern, is one of them. Bona knows, for example, that the student body of the Celebration School boasts more than one hundred former presidents of PTAs and PTSAs among the parents, and that parental involvement can also be a bit daunting to teachers, especially those who aren't used to it.

"Some parents are so involved, they want to run the school," she jokes. "The school is certainly not perfect," she admits, "but the issues are the same ones you'll find anywhere. This is real life."

"At the end of the day," says resident Jackson Mumey, who spearheaded the award-winning debate and speech program at the school, "my kids had a fabulous education." Daughter Megan is on a full academic scholarship at the University of Southern California, and son Mackenzie, a senior, is a nationally ranked debater. But Mumey also holds that part of the reason the education improved was because he and other parents started teaching, investing untold hours in making the school better.

To the Mumeys it was not so much that there were problems at the school. Or that the family's best friends moved out of town. Or that there was a period of four years where they and a neighbor didn't speak. Mumey, who runs his own business from home, thinks that the school controversy marked a critical change in the way The Celebration Company treated the town and its residents.

He believes that the press attendant on the school controversy unnerved the Disney company. "I love living here," he says in the well-modulated tones of the actor he once was, "and The Celebration Company has done a lot of great things. But as they got afraid, they began to reduce their own expectations."

Everyone's invited for a larger-than-life meal at the Waronka house, including three live canines and one inanimate Bob to make eating at home seem like a trip to the Big Boy.

"Celebration is an awesome place to live.

Find me someplace else that's better.

I don't think it's out there."

—*Susan Bona*

Not everyone has the same perspective. Patrick Carrin, who is pastor of the interdenominational Celebration Community Church, came to town as a project executive with Honeywell, one of Disney's original corporate strategic partners in creating Celebration. At first, he relates, his wife did not want to move to Celebration because it sounded too perfect and she feared that her family wouldn't fit in. Terry Carrin now works as a development officer of Celebration Health. According to her husband, she changed her mind when she realized that it was a real town with real people who had real problems.

Carrin, who says he has received a great deal of encouragement from The Celebration Company in his mission to build a roof over his congregation, is energetic in his delight at living here. "This is one of the finest places to live I've ever known," he says, voicing a positive outlook that is widespread among residents. "And I think the reason it is so fine is that Disney set the bar so high at the beginning. And they might not have achieved everything they set out to do, but thank God they tried!"

"In the beginning," he remembers, "a group of authentic visionaries put together a plan for this city. At a certain point it was time for the visionaries—say, the people in the Pentagon—to move on and create a vision for something new and to turn over their plan to a field general or tactical general to come in and implement the strategies."

The Celebration Company's former president, Perry Reader, had exactly that job between 1998 and 2004. He served as something of a lightning rod for the criticism of unhappy residents. On the other hand, he receives a great deal of credit from people like Pastor Patrick Carrin for the way the town works. "I respect the way he's developed this community," says Carrin, "and I have a lot of trust for him." Carrin also points out that the demands Reader has had to face from some of the residents have been extreme. "There were people here," remembers Carrin, "who thought that because they had trouble getting their houses built, they should get a free home."

Sue Bona also sticks up for Reader. "Look," says the Boston native, "anyone who has to make hard business decisions and finds themselves in the position of having to say no will be unpopular from time to time. I'm not the most popular person in the world with my employees sometimes."

Ironically, perhaps, the tempest over the school may have provided for a greater diversity of educational opportunities at Celebration, which already had a Montessori School as well as a fully professional day-care center, primarily for younger children. Parents who did not like the "watering down" of the original vision of the Celebration School opened a new, private school, the Navigator School, which offers enrichment classes of all kinds to children in town in addition to its own students. Some Celebration kids go to private and/or parochial schools nearby; some high-school kids participate in the international baccalaureate program at Gateway School in Kissimmee. There's also a large home-schooling network in town.

The opening of Celebration High School in August 2003 brought something to the town it had never had before: a football team and Friday-night games. Students come from Celebration and surrounding communities.

Meanwhile, Stetson University, which played a major role in the planning of the education system in Celebration, began operating a limited teaching center in town in 1996. Stetson found Celebration a good fit with its own educational mission. The building Stetson went on to open directly across the street from the K–12 in 2001—designed by the fast-track New York architecture firm Deamer + Phillips—helps fulfill the town's lifelong learning philosophy.

Ron Clifton, the Stetson Center's director, thinks that the problem with the school might not prove to have been such a bad thing in the long run. "The task for any community is to build a sense of community," says Clifton, a sociologist,

For a small community, the number of cultural opportunities is astonishing. The Royal Ballet of Celebration, which is housed at Celebration's Stetson University Center, is open to children from inside and outside the community.

"and community building is what's going on around Celebration. That's the tension and dynamic that's in the air. It's a process of change and development, and it's usually a very positive process."

The Stetson Center emerged as a valuable community resource. It offers MBA-degree courses in business and banking and, through its various partners, high-tech training and family counseling. Some five hundred people use the Stetson building every day. Among the various arts activities that take place under Stetson's extended roof are individual music lessons and the Royal Celebration Ballet, which offers classes for adults and children in modern, jazz, and classical dance.

The arts are extremely important in Celebration, as they tend to be in communities with a highly educated population. The Celebration Players, a theater group, presents a musical and nonmusical play or two each year. There's a singing group, too, and a classical concert series.

David Berelsman, who has "temporarily retired" to Celebration with his wife, Lyn, helps plan the Health Center's annual 10K/5K Walk/Run (Lyn is active with numerous groups, including the local Relay for Life, which benefits the American Cancer Society). David is also on the board of the Orlando opera. But Orlando, he says, "is just far enough away that people don't want to brave the traffic on I-4 to attend events up there." David and another Celebration resident who is active in the Orlando Philharmonic wanted to bring great music into town.

They started small, with a concert, and began to expand. Now there's a series. For the 2003 Founders' Day week, they organized a piano recital starring two well-known professionals from Stetson, a Celebration resident who was a concert pianist back home in Russia, and a fourteen-year-old phenomenon who's already studied in London.

There are also a couple of town-wide art shows each year, one dedicated to fine arts, the other more craft-oriented. Both make room available for local painters and

artisans. In fact, there is so much artistic activity in Celebration that a new umbrella organization, Celebration Arts, has been formed to coordinate such things as performance dates and use of the local facilities.

The coming together of the population in clusters defined by common interests was not just an accident of a particularly involvement-hungry group of home buyers (although they were that). Everything about the town's physical plant, from sidewalks and front porches to lot size and siting, encouraged residents to be neighborly. But the

There is an enormous range of activities in town—from art fairs and concert series to singing groups and dramatic societies like the Celebration Players

Celebration plan went even further toward meeting this increasingly perceived need for interconnection, building it into the town's administrative structure.

Celebration is not, strictly speaking, a town, despite its precedents and aspirations. "It looks like a town. It smells like a town. It works like a town," says Robert A.M. Stern, who concludes, therefore, "it's a town"—and in some sense he is absolutely correct. But, and it's a big but, Celebration does not have the legal status of an incorporated town. It is a tract of unincorporated Osceola County, a housing development, a planned community near Kissimmee, the county seat.

And running a town that is not a town but likes to think of itself as one called for a unique system of administration—both to supply all the necessities and niceties of a full-service neighborhood and to create the underpinning of a socially conscious community.

As it was finally shaped, there are essentially four entities responsible for running the "nontown" of Celebration. One is the county of Osceola, which is governed by a board of five elected commissioners serving four-year terms. Osceola County provides fire, emergency, and rescue services as well as policing, through the county sheriff's office. The Celebration School and High School are both county facilities, although The Celebration Company donated the land for both and contributed millions of dollars in curriculum and design enhancements.

Emergency services are provided by Osceola County from Fire Station No. 72 (formerly No. 94) in Celebration, home to the town's annual Rotary Club pancake breakfast fund-raiser.

"Scarcely eighteen months after the first family moved in, Celebration has become a ground for a luxuriant growth of scout troops, religious groups, and hobbyist clubs of every conceivable stripe."

—*Michael Pollan*

Overseeing "infrastructure improvements" are two Community Development Districts, authorized by the state of Florida as units of special-purpose local government. Common in the state, these CDDs were a matter of individual legislation until 1980, after which they became regulated under Chapter 190 of Florida's statutes. They exist to provide infrastructure—that is, such things as roadway lights, street sweeping, common-area landscaping, public parks, and trails—and to maintain the water utilities. The two CDDs are the Celebration CDD, which handles resident areas, and the Enterprise CDD, which has jurisdiction over the commercial property at the edges of the community.

CDDs have the power to float bond issues, which gives them access to financing not available through banks. "Between 1980 and 1986," says Gary Moyer, who has managed the Celebration CDDs, "there were about a dozen or so [CDDs] in the state. From 1986, with the

problems we had with savings and loan associations, they mushroomed and have become almost the norm in starting up new communities." Currently there are about 225 CDDs operating in Florida.

Moyer lists among the advantages of community CDDs the public scrutiny under which Florida law requires them to operate. All the meetings and records of the CDDs are public. Furthermore, he suggests, "projects that use CDDs are, generally speaking, better maintained, have a better quality, and are better amenitized than they would be if they hadn't been financed through CDDs."

In addition to the county and the CDDs, Celebration is governed by a bifurcated community association. It is comprised of the Celebration Residential Owners Association (CROA) and the Celebration Non-Residential Owners Association (CNOA), for rental apartments and commercial uses. They come together under a Joint Committee and are administered by Town Hall. The "Town Manager," Pat Wasson, is something of a mayoral figure in town, but she was not elected. She was hired by the five-member board of the community association, which until 2003 was controlled by The Celebration Company with three of five seats occupied by high-ranking Disney employees.

Virtually every activity at Celebration was begun by a Celebration resident and is run entirely by volunteers. Boy Scouts and Girl Scouts are only two of the myriad activities for school-age children.

Johnson Hall, the board room
of Town Hall, is the nerve center of
Celebration's governance actvities
(pictured: casting a ballot for CROA
board elections in September 2003).

Town Hall, which serves as a clearinghouse for most of the matters of community living in Celebration, has its hand in so many activities that it would be impossible to list them all. Town Hall, for example, oversees several key committees, including the Safety Committee and the Computer Network Committee. Its Architectural Review Committee is responsible for granting or denying permission for alterations and improvements throughout the residential areas of the town, and for helping unsuccessful petitioners to find alternative solutions. The Covenants Committee is charged with maintaining the numerous rules and regulations that apply to all the residential properties.

Other duties of Town Hall fall into the category of day-to-day details, including maintaining community network passwords and pool passes and serving as a kind of kiosk for information, as well as coordinating security and regulating trash collection. Town Hall is in charge of the town's Web site, The Front Porch, and the intranet, as well as the closed-circuit community TV station. Town Hall also publishes a monthly newsletter, the *Celebration News*, which serves as one of the town's two regular newspapers. The other, the *Celebration Independent*, was founded by town resident Alex Morton.

Town Manager Pat Wasson coordinates the activities of Town Hall and oversees its staff. She serves on numerous organizational committees and helps coordinate Celebration's countless community programs.

Each Halloween, the children of Celebration are invited to participate in a pumpkin-carving competition; finished, the illuminated jack-o'-lanterns ring the lake. OPPOSITE: Balance-beaming in a gymnastics class in the North Village Pavilion.

Socializing and fun are big parts of Town Hall's agenda, too. Annual town-wide events such as the Great Egg Hunt at Easter and the Pumpkin Carving Festival at Halloween are sponsored by Town Hall, and Town Hall is involved in a number of Founders' Day events and recreational programs for kids and teens. Town Hall even maintains a trailer stocked with all the supplies a group of neighbors might need to have a block party. Anyone who wants to can sign up to borrow it.

Town Hall administers Celebration's 27 acres of parks, with their swimming pools, tennis courts, basketball courts, volleyball courts, playgrounds, pavilions, and meeting facilities. It also coordinates a panoply of weekly classes (dog training, for example), clubs (yoga), and lessons (infant swimming and art). There is virtually no hour of any day that does not have at least one event scheduled through Town Hall.

One of the most innovative wings of Celebration's experimental administrative structure was the creation of the Celebration Foundation, a not-for-profit organization conceived as the nerve center for volunteerism and community building. Started with seed money from Disney, SunTrust Bank, and Kohler (one of Celebration's alliance members), the Foundation is now financed by fund-raising, donations, and fees taken from the sale of every home in town. The Foundation maintains a small office and runs a variety of community activities, such as orientation programs for new residents. It also publishes the Community Directory, the town's extremely useful phone book (it comes complete with street addresses, e-mail addresses, and the names of all the members of each household).

Block parties like this one are a popular activity in Celebration. In fact, so many of Celebration's residents wanted to organize block parties to bond with their neighbors that Town Hall now maintains a trailer fully stocked with all the basics, from tables and chairs to barbecue grills.

"A real sense of community can't develop in a vacuum," wrote Witold Rybczynski in the *New Yorker* in 1996, "and Disney seems to have gone out of its way to insure that Celebration will not become a hermetic place." In fact, the stated goal of the Celebration Foundation, which is run by a volunteer board, is community building "in Celebration, Osceola County, and the greater Central Florida area."

And although some of Celebration's near neighbors are skeptical, if not downright hostile to Celebration, the fact is that Celebration gladly extends its hand to the wider populace. "People around here don't know how many volunteers from Celebration work in Kissimmee and St. Cloud," says real estate broker Linda Goodwin-Nichols. The exuberant Goodwin-Nichols has lived in Osceola County for over thirty years and serves as a

Kissimmee City Commissioner as well as a trustee of the Celebration Foundation.

Fund-raising by the active Celebration Women's Club benefits Osceola County's shelter for battered women and their children. The Celebration Rotary Club is only one of a number of the new town's organizations that lends its muscle to Kissimmee's Give Kids the World, which houses children with life-threatening ailments and their families. Celebration's churches are open to anyone, of course, and so are the innumerable community activities, from the biannual porch-and-yard sales to the holiday observations

Face painting in Town Center during the town's annual Celebration of Fall.

on Easter, Memorial Day, Fourth of July, Halloween, and Christmas/Hanukkah.

Since its inception, many area organizations and individuals have been the recipients of the Foundation's financial or volunteer largesse. They include the Celebration Players (the resident theater group), the Boy Scouts, Sounds of Celebration (a singing group), the Celebration PTSA (that's a PTA with students added to the mix), Goodwill Industries, Habitat for Humanity, the Nature Conservancy, Foundation for Osceola Education, the Osceola County Children's Home, the Salvation Army, the Red Cross, United Way, March of Dimes, and many others.

The Celebration Foundation has a scholarship fund, bestows community service awards, and cosponsors *The View from Celebration*, a regularly scheduled program on Channel 12, the community station. It also hosts the Fourth of July Parade, a Spring Fling, and Founders' Day, and coordinates volunteers for the increasingly popular All-American Pie Festival. (In 2003 the Food Network ran

Celebration is the host of an annual Fourth of July parade and festival. Each December shopping season Market Street is showered with "snow." It's the only chance most of these kids will ever have to attempt a snow angel (or even a snow foam angel).

The Celebrators, the town's over-50 group, meets for *petanque* at Lakeside Park every Saturday morning; a French lawn-bowling game, *petanque* was introduced to Celebration by a British resident. There's an active Garden Club founded by a certified master gardener who also advises the Covenants Committee on landscaping and planting.

IN APPRECIATION OF
PEG OWENS
WHO FOUNDED
THE GARDEN CLUB OF
CELEBRATION
IN 1996

its Great American Pie Festival in Celebration, and the amateur grand-prize winner was a Celebration resident.)

The Foundation also sponsors bimonthly "Lights 'N' Lemonade" evenings. These are front-porch mixers where individual families agree to provide lemonade to anyone who stops by. It's already a town tradition, and a great place to meet new people in a leisurely setting with no agenda whatever except being sociable.

What is most inspiring about the multitude of activities in Celebration is that so many of them were started by individuals to meet personal needs. Peg Owens, a home-owner who had been certified as a master gardener by the state of Florida, started the Celebration Garden Club, whose current membership now boasts three master gardeners.

And resident Lisa Baird started the Women's Club. With her two children well established at school, Baird started looking outward for a way to get involved in the community. She wondered about an organization for women. "I went over to the Foundation office and asked if there was a Junior League or a women's club," she remembers, "and they said, 'No, but what a great idea—why don't you start one?' That was how it was in those days. No matter what you wanted to get involved in, you had to start it from scratch."

Baird posted a notice on the town's Internet bulletin board. She received one reply, from Risa Wight. Baird and Wight, who are now close friends, met for lunch and tossed around some ideas, considering, among others, the Junior League.

"But that was a problem because there were age restrictions," says Baird, "and Celebration had people in every age category. We wanted to be as inclusive as possible." The two women decided to found an affiliated chapter of the General Federation of Women's Clubs.

ABOVE: Members of the Chamber of Commerce prepare welcome baskets for new residents. BELOW: The bell ringers of the Presbyterian Church, the first congregation in town with its own building.

"People around here don't know how many volunteers from Celebration work in Kissimmee and St. Cloud—from the Women's Club providing juice for children at the women's shelter to the organizations that support Give Kids the World."

—Linda Goodwin-Nichols

Like their parent organization, the Celebration Women's Club is involved in political and social causes that primarily affect women and children.

The first year, the Women's Club had twelve members. They decided to create a Holiday Walk: each of the women would decorate her home for the year-end season, and they would charge a modest fee for other people in town to attend Saturday evening / Sunday afternoon open houses. That event has now become a town tradition. The club brought in $2,000 in its first year, and in 2003, the 120-member club raised close to $20,000 without having upped the price of admission.

Money from the Holiday Walk goes to scholarships for children in the Celebration School or children who live in Celebration but attend school elsewhere. The Women's

Club is also extremely active in its support of the Osceola County Help Now Women's Shelter, which is one of the organizations that receives the proceeds of the club's 2003 cookbook, *An American Celebration: Recipes and Traditions of Celebration, Florida.*

An American Celebration contains recipes from a variety of residents and celebrities, including George and Laura Bush, Jeb Bush, Bob and Elizabeth Dole, Michael Eisner, and Diane Sawyer. It also has menus from local chefs and by a certain ubiquitous Austrian restaurateur named Wolfgang Puck.

Many of the watercolor illustrations in the cookbook were created by painter Lynn Sands, who lives in Celebration with her husband and three children. Lynn's father, Rudy Nappi, a frequent Celebration visitor, was the original illustrator of the Hardy Boys and Nancy Drew books, and in her childhood Lynn served as the model for Nancy Drew.

The Garden Club now has a book in the works, too. It will be an illustrated guide to all the plants, flowers, trees, and shrubs that conform to the landscaping covenants of the town. (A member of the Garden Club serves on the Architectural Review Committee, since many of the improvements and changes homeowners would like to make involve issues of planting.) The new book is likely to be as widely used in Celebration as the Women's Club cookbook.

OPPOSITE: Women's Club members buy their weekly supply of juice and milk to take to the Help Now shelter for abused women in Osceola County. ABOVE AND BELOW: Three generations of women (Staci and Terri Haber and Terri's mother, Ila Titshaw) whip up some cookies from *An American Celebration*, a Women's Club cookbook that raises money for women's charities.

And in the way of such things (certainly in the way of Celebration), members of the Women's Club started a local chapter of the Red Hat Society, a social organization for women over the age of 50. Not to be excluded, a younger group started a Pink Hat Society, which lowers the age of membership to 40. Both groups, attired in appropriate headwear, meet for lunches and teas and "girls' nights out." It is not unusual in Celebration to meet someone who is active in the Women's Club and the Garden Club and the Red or Pink Hats and the Celebrators, the town's over-50 club, which targets retirees and senior citizens for civic, recreational, and social activities.

Mary Pfeiffer, a retired nurse, master gardener, and avid reader, was unhappy with the local county library and its space in the Celebration School. To her mind, it was too small, it wasn't open often enough, and it didn't necessarily provide the books she and her friends wanted to read. She began to find that others felt the same way.

Celebration boasts social organizations for every age group. Pictured are members of the local Red Hat Society meeting for tea in the home of Helen Baynes. There's a Pink Hat Society, too, for younger women. Seniors of both sexes can join the Celebrators.

Retired nurse Mary Pfeiffer (pictured at a
biweekly reading hour for preschoolers)
started a volunteer library run by
volunteers and stocked by donations.
Celebration has a toy library, too.

Pfeiffer, whose husband is a doctor in town, decided
to do in Celebration what Benjamin Franklin did in
Philadelphia: she started her own library. Town Hall
found a space for the project, a little-used room in a
community pavilion at Lakeside Park, downtown. She
found a carpenter who was willing to build shelves, and
no shortage of neighbors to donate books by the boxload.

The one-room library is now open almost every
day and is staffed by Pfeiffer and a group of dedicated
volunteers. It's a surprisingly professional organization, too.
Books are cataloged and rotated off the overstuffed
shelves. The library operates on a small budget from
cash donations and book sales and is now actually able
to acquire new books directly from publishers. The library
offers a biweekly reading group for preschoolers and a
summer reading program to help encourage kids to make
books a part of their vacation experience.

Like Epcot at Disney World, shopping and dining in Celebration are international affairs: Italian, Japanese, and Cuban foods are available, as well as traditional Southern and all-American fare.

As the town toddled on from infancy, the residents and The Celebration Company were able to begin working out conflicts with much less wear and tear. For aesthetic reasons, the covenants of the town did not allow any signs to be posted except for political purposes (a constitutional right), but some relocating homeowners wanted to post For Sale signs, so the community went about finding a solution. In the early days, for example, no one was permitted to put a For Sale sign on their property. The Celebration Company made an exception for its own properties, and residents began to think, quite rightly, that this was unfair.

A special task force was created at Town Hall. The ultimate compromise was that anyone selling a home in Celebration could post one sign on the property. The task force also recommended new covenants regarding the size and design and placement of the sign, but, as town manager Pat Wasson points out, "everyone is now on a level playing field."

Another area of concern to the residents of Celebration has been the mix of retail shops in the downtown area. "It's a great place to buy a loaf of bread or a diamond necklace," jokes Tod Joossens, who moved with his wife and children to Celebration to be near his father after the senior Joossens, a doctor, had a heart attack. What the downtown lacks, its critics feel, are things like a bookstore and a hardware store, friendly places to get needs met quickly, and where buying a pound of four-penny nails is also an occasion to chew the fat with friends. But the town is too small to support most of the service-oriented businesses the residents desire. Giant superstores like Home Depot, Target, and even Barnes and Noble operate not more than a 20-minute drive away. Restaurants do well in downtown Celebration, and they provide a variety of dining experiences at different price points. The retail shops that do manage to survive tend to be high-end antiques and gift shops that cater more to tourists than to locals.

Businesses of all kinds cater to Celebration, from clothing shops (including a boutique for kids) to a Sunday morning farmers' market. Claudine Andrews and Keith Albrizzi (OPPOSITE with their four kids) run NEVrland, the town's supplier of electric vehicles of all kinds, including scooters and Segways.

Still, new needs have been addressed in the evolution of businesses downtown. Claudine Andrews and her husband, Keith Albrizzi, found Celebration by accident. They were driving to the airport and got lost. They moved, with their young children to an apartment in Celebration without a very clear idea of how they would support themselves. They hit on the idea of renting cars from in front of the hotel. The idea was a good one, and worked well for the couple until they hit on another: electric vehicles.

Claudine and Keith, who have four school-age children, started NEVrland, a retail operation that sells and rents electric vehicles, including scooters for kids and teens and NEVs. Neighborhood Electric Vehicles, as they are officially called, look and function like golf carts and can seat two or four people along with some packages and groceries. Celebration now ranks number one in the nation for per capita ownership of electric vehicles. There are even NEV-only parking spaces in town, complete with recharging points.

Celebration is also a designated test market for personal electric transport—more specifically, for Segways, a two-wheel mode of mobility that is operated while standing up. Claudine and Keith distributed two hundred of them the first week of business. In fact, NEVrland has been so successful that it is beginning a franchise operation.

Most residents are delighted with the alternatives to ozone-eating gas-guzzlers. "To me," says Mary Ann Kinser, a retired college administrator, "driving is like cleaning the bathroom—it's one of those things in life you have to do, but it's a chore."

After his wife passed away, Dick Rianhard (RIGHT) became a leading force in the creation of a meditative Memorial Garden. The first plaque, that of Eleanor Rianhard, was given to Dick by fellow members of the organizing committee.

A somewhat trickier issue was the matter of burial. Some residents of the town wanted Disney to provide a cemetery, and the local churches asked the company to do so. Disney declined. But in October 1997, just six weeks after she and her husband moved into their Lake Evalyn home, Eleanor Rianhard died on a fall foliage trip to Asheville, North Carolina. "She was never sick a day in her life," says surviving husband Dick Rianhard, who now lives in the upscale Mirasol apartment complex. "She went to sleep and never woke up."

The Rianhards, originally from Maine, moved to Celebration because they wanted an active second half and were attracted by the value the town placed on community. When Eleanor died, the support was immediate and widespread. And Rianhard is effusive in his words of gratitude for Celebration employees like Marilyn Waters, the former PR officer of The Celebration Company, and for neighbors who came to his aid.

Eager to do something to commemorate his wife, Dick joined the Garden Club—he was the only man—and began to lobby for a Memorial Garden. The club persuaded Nelsons' Florida Roses, whose nursery is north of Orlando, in Apopka, Florida, to donate rosebushes. But, Rianhard says, "Perry Reader told me to dream big."

A retired engineer with his own business, a former fighter pilot, and the sole surviving member of a three-hundred-person test group of terminal cancer patients (he lost a leg to the disease), Rianhard is not a man who backs down from a challenge. He started a committee to plan the Memorial Garden. It took two years, with the active support of Reader and The Celebration Company, but the Memorial Garden is now a reality. "It's beautiful," says Rianhard, who seems to have a permanent twinkle in his eye. "It's a place to think and meditate, and it's a garden." The first plaque to be installed in the Memorial Garden was that of Eleanor Rianhard; it was a gift to Dick from fellow members of the Memorial Garden planning committee.

The Rev. Patrick Wrisley (BELOW) is not what you might expect of a Presbyterian minister. He was the force behind the construction of the town's first church building, which he opens to the community for meetings and concerts that need a large hall.

The rituals of life and death are important in any community, and religion is as essential here to some residents as it was for those who lived in the historic communities that inspired the place. The master planners of Celebration had, naturally enough, included steepled churches in their original design notions, but Disney did not think the Mouse could be in the business of religious architecture. They did go so far as to leave several small parcels of their land empty for the possible construction of churches or synagogues at a later date.

The absence of worship buildings did not in the least daunt those who wanted to gather, however, and various religious groups have been convening in Celebration since Founders' Day of 1996. Among the congregations that have been established are the Celebration Community Church (interdenominational), which held the town's first religious service during Founders' Day 1996; the Celebration Community Presbyterian Church; the Seventh-Day Adventists, who hold services on Saturday at the chapel inside Celebration Health; the United Parish of Celebration, another interdenominational Protestant church; and the Celebrate Family Church, which meets at the AMC theater.

Although the Celebration Community Church is considering a site for a church, only one congregation has as yet been successful in mobilizing its members to create their own sanctuary. The Celebration Community Presbyterian Church, the largest of the Protestant churches in town, bought one of the small parcels in the center of town.

The Rev. Patrick Carrin and family say grace before dinner.

The church was built through the contributions of its members and the mother church as well as other benefactors. Its pastor is the Rev. Patrick Wrisley, a garrulous, bearded bear of a man who drives a motorcycle, smokes cigars, and serves as a bit of a thorn in the side of The Celebration Company. He's as irreverent as he is generous of spirit, and his everyone-welcome church is based on the principle of universal love.

Wrisley is a respected community leader whose church is used frequently for town meetings and other gatherings. He also offers up the sanctuary for interfaith services for Thanksgiving and for memorial services on 9/11. While most of the communicants at the Presbyterian church live in Celebration, about 30 percent, Wrisley estimates, live outside its boundaries.

Wrisley has an idealistic side as well as a pragmatic one. He thinks that spirituality should have been stated as a sixth cornerstone of the original Celebration master plan and that Disney should be more friendly to church-building. (As of 2004, another congregation, Rev. Patrick Carrin's Celebration Community Church, is exploring the possibility of acquiring another tract of Disney land to build its church.)

Looking down the list of religious organizations that routinely meet in Celebration, you'll also find the Celebration Jewish Congregation, which is affiliated with the Reconstructionist branch of Judaism. Its spiritual leader, Brian Levine, actually came to Celebration to help design

The Jewish community of Celebration is small and does not yet have either a building or a rabbi. For High Holy Days, they meet in Heritage Hall (Yom Kippur of 2003 is pictured).

and run the Celebration Community Network. "Although the Jewish Community in town is small," Levine says, "about 100 or 125 turn up for the congregation's Hanukkah party and High Holy Day observances." Levine looks forward to a time when the Jewish congregation can build or acquire its own space, which he believes will help strengthen the temple. Meanwhile, some of Celebration's Jews feel the 25-minute drive to the South Orlando Jewish Center is worth the effort in order to be in a building of their own.

It was the Habers, the town's first residents, who approached Levine about starting a congregation, although he is not a rabbi (he does speak Hebrew, however, and is well tutored in the Torah and religious rituals). The Habers' son, Brandon, had the town's first bar mitzvah, at Lakeside Park; sister Staci's bat mitzvah was a bit more glamorous (the family flew off to the Virgin Islands).

Because the Jews in town are a clear minority, a certain amount of education was in order, particularly with respect to the Celebration School. "There have been issues," says Levine, kindly. PTA elections were once scheduled for a major Jewish religious holiday, for example. But the biggest problem of being so small a minority, Levine feels, is the lack of support. A project director with SAIC, the consulting firm, Levine travels frequently to large cities. "In Atlanta," he relates, "there are a dozen synagogues and the kosher section in the Publix is a whole aisle. There's a real feeling of being part of the community at large."

Most of the town's clergy meet together regularly in the spirit of ecumenism and to foster spirituality in general. The only local padre who refuses to attend is head of one of the more fundamentalist Protestant churches. He will not join the group because of the presence of a Jewish leader and an imam, who administers to the town's Muslim population. "We keep praying for him," says Patrick Wrisley. The situation is particularly remarkable, since instances of open prejudice in Celebration are extremely rare.

Celebration has some diversity, but it is not yet as heterogeneous as was predicted or as some residents would like. The popular notion that Celebration is white, rich, Republican, and Christian is not entirely true, but there are statistics to back the town's critics.

A map of the local voting precincts hangs in the home office of Florida State Representative Randy Johnson, who lives in Celebration with his wife, Darlene. In addition to being a political wife and mother of two teenagers, Darlene makes natural cosmetics from herbs and flowers that grow in town. Daughter Brooke is on the high school volleyball team; son Jordan has been working as a cashier at the nearest supermarket to earn money to buy a car.

Johnson is a Republican in a Republican-dominated district (No. 41, the "tourist corridor"). There are small pockets of Democrats here and there, but by and large, his constituency is pure GOP. Celebration, he notes, not only votes Republican by a greater majority than its Republican neighbors (a solid 80 percent), but it votes in greater numbers, realizing the town's potential clout with bodies as well as campaign contributions.

But it was not so much the Republicanism that drew the Johnsons to Celebration as the effusive hospitality. While running for office, the Johnsons did what politicians do in Florida: They went out and knocked on doors to solicit support one voter at a time.

"In Celebration, not only did people let us in and listen to my philosophy and my agenda, they'd walk me next door, or to every house on the block. At some houses they didn't even knock. They just stuck their heads in the door and shouted a greeting." Johnson went to one home that was quite receptive. The homeowner loaned the Johnsons his NEV, which he hung with Randy Johnson election posters. The resident was then-banker Charlie Rogers, who now runs the Celebration Foundation and is involved in countless local activities.

There are, of course, donkeys among the elephants. And local doctor, John Pfeiffer, a family practitioner who

The environment is extremely important to the planners and residents of Celebration, who live side by side with many species, some of them endangered. Landscape choices are outlined in the *Pattern Book*.

runs an old-fashioned office in downtown Celebration and actually makes the occasional house call, is an outspoken Libertarian.

As for wealth, this issue is trickier. Realtor Sonny Buoncervello, a longtime Osceola County resident, moved with his wife, Becky, and their children to Celebration from a nearby high-end community. He estimates that the average home in Celebration costs $50,000 to $100,000 more than comparable properties nearby—if you can find them. This is widely known as the "Celebration premium," which virtually everyone who lives here says is worth the money. When you buy a house in Celebration, the collective wisdom runs, you are buying more than a house; you're buying a lifestyle worth the price tag.

According to statistics, the average stand-alone home in Celebration is valued at around $300,000 and in Osceola County about $150,000. The average in Celebration, of course, is driven upward by the presence of $1 million properties, many of them owned by premature retirees. Additionally, there is the common Celebration situation of being "house rich and cash poor."

"You go into some of these lovely homes," says Randy Johnson, "and there's no furniture inside, because the family's financial resources are all going into living here."

"The biggest myth I would like to dispel," says Terri Haber, "is the idea that we are all wealthy here. It's much more accurate to say that residents of Celebration are solidly middle class, while the general population of Osceola County lags farther behind." Furthermore, although there are more at-home moms and dads in Celebration than in most American neighborhoods, many households here require two adults to work full-time to pay for all the perks.

In fact, the range of property costs in Celebration is one of its strong points, embracing apartments, condominiums, and cottages as well as substantial five- and six-bedroom houses and some quite stately golf-course-facing homes.

While Disney came under fire for not working harder to provide affordable housing for low-income families, diversity of housing has attracted a wide variety of renters and owners. There are traditional families, certainly, and couples who are retired, just starting out, and in between. The town has a fair number of single people, too—unmarried, divorced, or widowed, both men and women, gay and straight. There are single mothers and fathers; some of the town's children have special needs. There are adoptive families, extended families, blended families ("Yours, Mine, and Ours"), even gay families, some of them raising children.

"I wouldn't want our names published in a book," says one lesbian parent, "but my partner and I are both active in the community. I'm a member of the Rotary Club. We go to social events as a couple, and people seem to accept it."

Those garage apartments so popular in Celebration provide convenient housing for elders, so three-generation families are easy to find, even if all the generations don't live at the same address. Mary Ann and Paul Kinser are both retired college administrators. They live on Celebration Avenue across the street from Mirasol, an up-market apartment complex. Paul's mother, Madge Kinser, is an active member of the Celebrators and, in her late nineties, the town's eldest resident. The Kinsers moved to Celebration in part because of the chance it gave the extended family for Madge to live independently. She's on her own, but near enough to her son and daughter-in-law that they can look after her.

Extended families are common in
Celebration. The three-generation
Joossens clan—grandparents Richard
and Alice, parents Tod and Christine,
and kids Connor, Parker, Ramsey,
and Hayden—live in two homes.

There's at least one four-generation family, too. Susan
Bona (née Whooley) is married to Bill Bona, who runs an
annual golf tournament benefiting the school's Booster
Club, which provides funds for the sports teams. The
Bonas had no intention of moving to Celebration from
Ft. Lauderdale, but they were Disney Vacation Club
members and just happened to be in town the day of the
original lottery. They entered the lottery "on a lark" and
pulled number three for town houses.

Now the Bonas operate the Celebration Town Tavern,
which they hope functions as the "Cheers" of Celebration.
There are two Bona teenagers, Jeremy and Jianna; Susan's
parents (Janet and Jack Whooley) live in town, as does her
grandmother. The Health Center's Des Cummings observes
that advances in health care and the ever-increasing life
expectancy of Americans will make the twenty-first century
the first time in human history when five-generation
families are not only feasible but taken for granted.

Some families have extended laterally as well as down
the generations, with adults following siblings who have
settled here. It's far from unusual to meet people whose
sisters and brothers, nieces and nephews, aunts and uncles
live just a few blocks away, adding the kind of literal
familiarity that long-established towns have developed
over decades. Susan Bona's sister, Linda, and her son,
William, also live in town.

And then there is race. Celebration is not all white. It
has members of many ethnic and racial groups. Mixed
marriages are not uncommon in Celebration, nor are mixed-
race families, thanks to an active adoptive subcommunity.
But Celebration is clearly far more Caucasian than Osceola
County. According to the 2000 Census, the racial makeup
of the town is "93.57% White, 1.72% African American,
0.26% Native American, 2.41% Asian, 0.00% Pacific
Islander, 1.02% from other races, and 1.02% from two or
more races; 7.60% of the population are Hispanic or
Latino of any race."

By 2003, the numbers had changed slightly in the
direction of greater diversity, and it is quite clear from walking around the town that it is home to blacks (African-
American and Afro-Caribbean), Latinos, Asians and South

People of all ages enjoy Celebration on their own terms. ABOVE: Kids Night Out at the Heritage Hall pool.

OPPOSITE: Retired librarian Dorothy Johnson, an independent octogenarian.

Asians, Middle Easterners, and others. Sonny Patel is a Brit of Indian heritage whose business is commercial real estate. He has two teenagers, Devin and Janisha, both of whom are golfing at near-professional levels. But Patel is not satisfied that Celebration's diversity is yet utopian; for this concerned golf father, there is still much work to be done before the ethnic mix of Celebration is comfortable.

One of Celebration's favorite residents is the prodigious Dorothy Johnson, a former teacher and retired librarian in her late eighties. Johnson, an African-American, lives alone in North Village in an apartment filled with Afrocentric art, memorabilia, and collectibles. She's an avid jazz fan and is active in an organization dedicated to preserving American Negro spirituals. She was in charge of the volunteer library's summer reading project and gets around town on a three-wheeled seated "bicycle."

Johnson also volunteers as a mentor/tutor to high school students. But not in Celebration. Instead she travels to Orlando, sometimes taking the bus, which can take hours, although there are often others in town who are happy to drive her there. And why does she travel so far to tutor? "I figure that the young people in Celebration have all the parental help they need. I wanted to go where I could do the most good."

Vicki Puntonet, who is of Latin descent and who hails from Coral Gables, moved to Celebration with her husband, Narciso, so that their two kids, Ilian and Cassidy, would have the same kind of healthy childhood she and her husband enjoyed. Vicki went to work at the Village Mercantile, the Market Street clothing store, which was opened by Dottie and Jerry Matheson in 1996 (it was also home to Orville, a much-beloved Vietnamese potbellied

pig). When the Mathesons were ready to retire, they offered the business to Vicki; the Puntonets and another couple agreed to form a partnership to buy the place.

Among Vicki's best friends are Sarai Cowin, another Latina. Cowin was raised in the South Bronx, a notoriously difficult and dangerous place to grow up; her motive for moving to Celebration was to provide her two daughters, Erica and Jennifer, with a different kind of experience. Cowin, who serves as the first president of the high school PTSA, is married to Dr. Richard Cowin, a podiatrist who is also a rabbi. Neither Puntonet nor Cowin feels that there is a problem with diversity in town and don't think anything in particular needs to be done to foster greater diversity. It will come, they believe, as does Dorothy Johnson, with time.

But how can Celebration communicate to people of color that they are truly welcome? One of Celebration's real estate agents, Dawn Thomas, is herself black (she was born in Trinidad). She moved to town with her son, Eddie, in 1996 and worked for The Celebration Company and Town Hall before settling

on real estate. The stories Dawn tells about life in Celebration are the same stories one hears from everyone in town: the people in Celebration care about their neighbors, and those neighbors happen to come in all kinds of colors.

At one point, Thomas had an automobile accident and broke her foot. Friends, neighbors, acquaintances rushed to help, bringing meals and watching after her son, who was one of the school's first star athletes. "To this day," says Thomas, "people who used to go to basketball games to watch Eddie play stop me on the street and ask how he's doing."

Thomas has lived, she says, in Miami and Brooklyn and in Tennessee and has seen "all kinds of ways people have for dealing with each other. I am certain that this town can work for anyone who lives here. I know that if I have a problem, I can go to anyone in this community for help and they'll say what do you need? They'll even come before I ask. They'll come and say, 'I hear you might need some help, what can I do?'"

The Cowin family: teenagers Erica and Jennifer, Sarai (first president of
the Celebration High School PTSA), and husband Richard, a rabbi as well as a doctor.

Kids gather paper leaves at the annual Market Street Autumn Leaf Festival (the leaves are then used in school craft projects).

Resident Wendy McNally on the porch of her own home with daughter Emma.

One of the signs of Celebration's maturity is a softening of the lines. Certainly, the "love it or leave it" mentality that was common in the early days has changed. Nowadays, a mellower community manages to put up with problems, or at least with issues they see as problems. Charles Eldredge, a video producer who now works as a real estate agent and who has served on the CROA board, has taken issue with several decisions of The Celebration Company. He believes, for example, that the company has revised its density projections to include too many apartments. "That's an issue for me," he says.

But Eldredge loves Celebration, as does his family (wife, Jan, and kids, Jamie, Chase, and Savannah). They've moved three times in town to find the place they could retire in. "We bought a house with a master suite on the ground floor so that we could still be living in it in forty years," says Charlie, who helped start the Cub Scouts when his son came home from school wanting to join. Both father and son have graduated to the Boy Scouts.

Interestingly, there are quite a few people who came to Celebration, left for one reason or another, and then came back. There are enough of them that they have their own name, boomerangs. Mark Robinson is one of the boomerangs. He moved to Celebration with his wife, Teresa, and their kids in May 2001. At first, he says, Celebration seemed too artificial, and the couple wasn't all that attracted to it. But daughter Bailey was about to enter second grade, and the Robinsons were impressed by the school and its facilities.

"If your child plays an instrument, they have a great band room," says Robinson. "If they like art, there are real clay ovens."

As things worked out, though, he accepted a job back up north (he was born in Jamaica but raised in the Northeast). The family moved out of Celebration in December of the same year they moved in. It wasn't long, however, before they started missing Celebration.

"We decided to follow our hearts," says Robinson, who has served on the town's Safety Committee and coaches Celebration's children's soccer

Among Celebration's numerous prodigies are Devin and Janisha Patel, who are both potential professional golfers.

group (his son, Max, is an avid player). "We had only lived here for a few months, but it was the only place we thought of as home." Now the volleyball-playing dad, who bikes to school with his kids several times a week, is starting his own business, a Caribbean catering service that specializes in jerk cuisine. Locals who have tasted his cooking at fund-raising events for the Brownies are sure Mark will be successful.

In its early years, the community began to establish certain rituals of interconnection that were related to the spanking-new downtown. Celebration is one of the few planned communities around America where dozens of neighbors are likely to be found from early morning and throughout the day, clustered at the indoor and outdoor tables at Barnie's Coffee and Tea or the nearly adjacent Sherlock's, an authentic English tearoom. The town is small enough that residents can easily scoot over to either of these venues for a brief chat or leisurely klatch with friends. Friendships in town develop across all the lines that remain uncrossed in many places in America.

Many of Celebration's residents have interesting stories; some are even well known in their fields. Former U.S. Congresswoman Pat Schroeder has a home here, as does PGA golfer Robert Gamez. Hank Wake, whose wife is Mary, is actually Chaplain (COL) Henry E. Wake, former Colonel of the Regiment and one of the highest-ranking chaplains in the U.S. Army.

It's not the kind of group to be attracted to most housing developments. "There are a lot of type A characters in town," jokes one of them. It is unlikely that any developer could provide the ideal town for each of the ten to twelve thousand people who will someday live in Celebration. But because it was Disney pioneering corporate sponsorship of a neotraditional town, everything that happened in Celebration became a matter of national concern.

Jackson Mumey's bid for the Osceola County School Board, for example, was covered in the *New York Times* and the *Los Angeles Times*. "How many other local school board elections in Florida do you think they covered?" he asks rhetorically.

It wasn't only the press and individuals invested in Disney (literally or figuratively, positively or negatively) who had their eyes on the development of Celebration. The world of architecture and planning was also watching, as were key governments. Would this private corporation working out of essentially self-serving (profit-driven) motives be able to create in Celebration the kind of community that no private developer or municipal entity was able or, for that matter, even interested in creating?

Many of the town's early struggles were recorded in two books that were published early in the town's history. *Celebration U.S.A.: Living in Disney's Brave New Town* was written by husband-and-wife duo Douglas Frantz and Catherine Collins; *The Celebration Chronicles: Life, Liberty, and the Pursuit of Property Value in Disney's New Town* was written by Andrew Ross, a New York University sociologist who grew up in Greenwich Village.

Frantz and Collins lived two doors away from Lisa and Scot Baird. "That book is so negative about

Celebration," says Lisa, "and this is such a positive place. I mean, I was at some of the same events that Doug and Catherine describe, and that's not how I remember them at all." Most who knew them agree, however, that Catherine Collins made great chocolate chip cookies. "I'll give her that," says Lisa Baird.

"When intellectuals disparage New Urbanist developments like Celebration as 'fake,'" wrote Kurt Anderson in the *New Yorker* in 1999, "what really seems to bother them is that talented, energetic members of their taste and educational caste are no longer abstaining from taking their part in the great postwar American architectural project, the building of suburbs, and have instead created a movement to reform suburbs, to make them more like old American towns where people walk and mingle. Celebration's 'fakery'—its small scale, its density, its hidden garages, its pre-mall commercial core—is in the service of a coherent vision as opposed to the adulation of developers' cost-efficient shortcuts and aesthetic bad habits that produce the random, sprawling, ghastly 'real' suburbs of the late twentieth century.

"Celebration," Anderson concluded, and many agree, ". . . is vastly superior, aesthetically and probably spiritually, to ninety-nine percent of the new housing developments in America."

Founders' Park, adjacent to Celebration School, is bricked with the names of the town's families.

OPPOSITE: Teenagers on a scavenger hunt during Founders' Day weekend.

4. LOOKING

FORWARD

By the summer of 2003, Disney was making the segue from its role as developer and had shifted into transfer mode. By the end of that year, The Celebration Company thought, Disney's participation in the affairs of the residential areas of Celebration would be minimal. The Mouse would sell its remaining town assets, the golf course, for example, and the downtown Market Street area, and turn over control of the community assets, such as the parks, etc., to CROA, the home-owners association.

Mike Gaw's NEV during the 2003 campaign for the CROA board of directors (Gaw was one of two winners from a field of eight). OPPOSITE: An election volunteer guards the ballot box.

CROA assembled a group of residents to create a transition team that would review the books on the community's holdings as well as the terms and covenants that govern life in Celebration. Part of this process involved recasting the sometimes convoluted legal language of the covenants to be more accessible to laymen and generally less ambiguous.

Mike Gaw, a retired U.S. Army Reserve major general who is active with his wife, Pattie, in Gaw Realty Services, agreed to head the committee. "The Committee," says Pat Wasson, the town manager, "worked intensely for six weeks to clear the way to a seamless transfer of power from Disney [the developer] to CROA [the homeowners association]."

As part of the process, elections to the five-member CROA board, scheduled for September 2003 for the seat of resident Rod Owen, whose term was expiring, took on a special resonance. For the first time since the creation of CROA, two residents would be elected to the board, one to the single vacating seat, and another to a seat previously occupied by a member of the Company's staff. In other words, the board would have a three-to-two resident majority for the first time. And although Disney maintains some veto power over decisions, the likelihood of using them, Perry Reader suggests, is minimal. "It's their town now," he says of the residents. By 2005, the board is scheduled to expand to seven members, all of them elected from among Celebration's resident owners.

No fewer than eight qualified owners filed petitions to run for the two 2003 positions. *The Celebration Independent*, which tends to be highly suspicious of Disney if not downright hostile, published the answers to a list of questions the paper's publisher, Alex Morton, sent to all the candidates. One of those questions pointedly asked if there was any business relationship whatsoever between the individual candidates and any Disney affiliate. There were none.

Surprisingly," says Pat Wasson in her Town Hall office, "it was a highly energetic election, with campaigning and posters like we've never had here before." And although only two of the eight highly regarded men and women who ran for the CROA board could be elected, "the good news," Wasson points out, "is that the people who didn't win in 2003

have higher name recognition should they decide to run again in a future election. We're blessed to have that many people who want to work that hard to help run their community."

After the votes were counted in September 2003, the two new board members announced were Mike Gaw and Pam Shaw, a Celebration activist and Celebration School PTSA president who had, like Gaw, also served on the transition team. Mike Mekdeci, director of liaison programs for The Celebration Company, would relinquish his company seat; Perry Reader and Matthew Kelly, vice president for real estate development and operations, would remain on the CROA board.

The transfer of control of Celebration from The Celebration Company to CROA within a time frame of five to ten years had always been part of the design of the Celebration business and governance plan. But even though the withdrawal of the developer was both natural and inevitable, residents had a wide variety of reactions to the moment. To some, it was good riddance to a micromanaging landlord. Others lauded the opportunity to run the town themselves, believing that the resident-majority CROA board would be more responsive to residents' needs. While others felt a wave of panic, as if they were being abandoned.

"I have to laugh when someone asks me if I know Disney is selling off its holdings in Celebration," says Internet executive Rob Wight, who lives with his wife and kids in a stately white-columned home at the end of Longmeadow Park. "I say, 'Of course I know. They sold some of it to me.'"

One of the first signs that Disney would keep the interests of the residents in the forefront of their transfer of assets was the sale of Celebration Golf Course in the fall of 2003. Among the conditions of the sale were that the course would remain public, keeping its access at the maximum, and that the course would maintain itself as a green space between the northern limits of the residential neighborhoods and the commercial district along Celebration Boulevard. The Celebration Company waited for a buyer willing to accept these conditions, finally reaching a $6.5 million agreement with C. S. Golf Partners LLC, a consortium of golf-minded businessmen.

"[This] leadership team," says Matthew Kelly, "brings four decades of experience in golf management and has a keen understanding of the role of Celebration Golf Course in the community."

In addition to Celebration Golf Course, which has been given four stars by *Golf Digest,* C. S. Golf Partners owns and manages six other courses in Florida and Canada. Among the principals are David Creighton, former NHL player and a golf course developer since the 1960s, as well as his son, Class-A PGA player David Creighton, Jr., who lives in Celebration and who was named director of the course.

The same care went into finding the right buyer for the Market Street shopping area, which was announced early in 2004. "The Celebration Company, a real estate development division of The Walt Disney Company," ran the company's press release, "has sold Celebration's town center…to Lexin Capital, a private real estate investment company. The Celebration Company is changing its business to concentrate on selling the remaining commercial land and the town center needs an owner who will focus long-term on its growth, management and operations."

As conditions of the sale, Lexin Capital agreed to retain and uphold the architectural design standards established by The Celebration Company. In addition, Lexin agreed to support Celebration's tradition of town center community events, such as Founders' Day and Fourth of July festivities.

"Lexin Capital has admired Celebration and its town center for many years and is delighted to purchase such an outstanding mixed-used property," said Metin Negrin, president of Lexin Capital. "We look forward to strengthening Market Street's position in Celebration and becoming an active member of the community."

Lexin's purchase encompasses 18 acres containing 16 retail shops, 6 full-service restaurants, more than 94,000 square feet of commercial office space, 105 private apartments, and 3 land parcels. In total, says the Lexin Web site, the property contains 273,000 square feet of Class A office, retail, and multifamily space as well as 6.8 acres of land.

Some of that land is the parcel now used as a parking lot between the Presbyterian church and

As The Celebration Company began to transfer control of the town to the residents, it began to sell its own holdings, including the golf course.

Lakeside Park, which may eventually contain another block of commercial space, although it may also be developed for further residences.

Oddly, since the many rules and covenants and the program of gentle persuasion Town Hall operates to enforce them (the so-called "porch police") seem to be so odious to outsiders, one of the most often stated concerns about the sale of downtown is the fear that Lexin will not maintain Disney's high standards and that CROA will not be as active in making sure the rules are equitably and universally applied.

While the original enormous shopping center west of Intersate 4 has been tabled indefinitely (although developing the property is still an active possibility), The Celebration Company planned for a new shopping zone, which is being developed by Unicorp National Developments. Water Tower Place, a shopping center designed by the Cooper Robertson office, opened in 2004 at the intersection of Celebration Avenue and U.S. 192.

Like Celebration, Water Tower Place was designed in an indigenous vernacular style. The center will be anchored by a large Goodings supermarket, the chain that has maintained a Market Street presence since 1996, and contain shops, restaurants, a bank, and a service station. And, happy news for many residents, it will be reachable from Celebration by foot, by bike, and by NEV (allowed on roads where the speed limit is 35 miles per hour or below).

Further home building in Celebration has been contracted to Arvida and other builders. By late 2003, Arvida had cleared the land and begun building homes in Artisan Park, the last of the residential neighborhoods to be completed in Celebration. The homes were already selling for prices ranging from "the $200,000s" to over $800,000 before the models were even complete.

Still to be built are an as-yet undetermined number of new hotels. They will go up on two sites in the commercial corridor (one on each side of World Drive, a direct route to Disney World) and an additional secluded parcel that has been acquired by Four Seasons Hotels and Resorts, one of the world's leading operators of luxury hotels.

Possibly the greatest hope for the town of Celebration in the long run is the new Celebration High School. Osceola County opened the school's $40 million doors in August 2003.

"Osceola approached us," recalls Perry Reader, and said, in effect, "'We need a new high school, and your kids are going to have to go to it to make the numbers work, so we think you should donate the land.'" Many residents of Celebration resisted the abbreviation of their cherished K–12 into a K–8. The high school would be larger and the kids would be coming from outside of Celebration.

Travel to school was now a matter of concern, as was transportation for the kids who came to town by bus: could the county, or could Celebration, afford the buses that make it possible for students to come into town and stay after school for the many events that enrich the high school experience?

"We are working overtime to make sure that the kids who come here from outside Celebration know that this is their school, too," says State Legislator Randy Johnson. And the bus program for afternoon activities is the key to the success of intramural sports and other activities.

Another concern for Celebration parents and students alike was that the students from Celebration, who had grown up in a small, active community with overwhelming parental involvement in their education, would soon be going to school with a very different group of kids, many of them from less affluent, more transient families. There was a fear that the standard of the high school would drop and that children and teens who had worked so hard to build the K–12 into an A-level institution, might begin to fall off their academic performance.

Others, however, see the new high school as an opportunity, a challenge rather than a problem. The advantages are obvious. For one thing, the school had a design tweaking by Graham Gund, one of Disney's favored architects, which makes it aesthetically more interesting than standard-issue high schools. The larger school would also offer greater opportunities in academic subjects as well as after-school programs and sports, like football. The Celebration School had never had a

The landmark at right gave its name to the new Water Tower Place shopping center at the intersection of Celebration Avenue and U.S. 192.

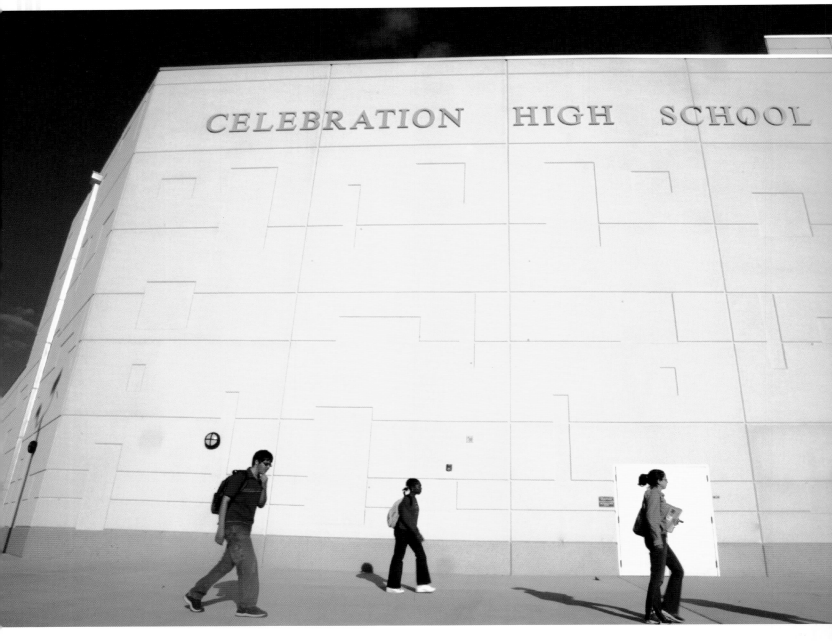

Architect Graham Gund helped design the new Celebration High School. Some homeowners are hoping to organize a private alternative.

football team until the opening of the new high school. One life preserver of continuity for students was the retention of John Bushey as principal of the high school (a role he continues from the K–12).

But the high school also represents an opportunity for some up-close-and-personal interaction between the people of Celebration and their neighbors in Kissimmee.

Personifying that hope is the first Parent/Teacher/Student Association president for the high school, Sarai Cowin. Having had the kind of childhood that many of the incoming students are having now, she may be in a unique position to bridge any distrust from both sides of the Celebration property line.

"Some of the notion that Celebration gets everything," says Randy Johnson, "is that this community provides for itself. Not every community can afford to do what Celebration can do, but ultimately communities have to provide for themselves."

One of the things that some residents would like to provide for themselves is incorporated status as a town or city. Another, some parents insist, is a private high school. And a committee has been formed by Celebration residents to explore that possibility.

Meanwhile, Disney is not entirely leaving town, as some fear. Its influence is not only present in the physical and social design of the town; they are maintaining a development office, too. The new focus of the Disney employees in Celebration will be on the commercial strip between downtown and the high school, which is only beginning to be sold.

So, is Celebration a success?

It might be a premature question. After all, the town is not yet even fully built at this point, or fully populated. But there are some good indicators that the town is successful by many criteria.

Certainly it has met a market demand, having tapped a need in the population that surprised a good number of business and cultural analysts. The rate of sales in Celebration has been faster than anticipated, precipitating the transition from The Celebration Company to the Celebration Residential Owners Association earlier than predicted. And homes have sold for more than was foreseen as property values continue to rise, particularly at the lower end of the price scale. Disney has set consecutive annual records for home sales.

The Disney company will certainly realize a profit from its huge financial commitment to Celebration. Disney's rate of return is expected, as was planned, to be far smaller than is usually demanded by the executives who run Disney. ("Believe me," Michael

The new high school brought a host of new opportunities to Celebration's young people. Teams are known as the Celebration Storms.

Eisner has said, "if all we wanted to do was make money, there would have been a lot of easier ways to do it.")

Furthermore, the town has won several prominent awards, including two 1998 awards from the American Society of Landscape Architects and the 1996 Development of the Year award from the National Association of Industrial and Office Properties. Celebration was also named as one of twenty-six projects to be included in the mammoth *Great Planned Communities*, published by the Urban Land Institute (ULI) in 2001.

The ULI—the preeminent, multidisciplinary real estate forum in the United States—is dedicated to providing leadership in the use of land to enhance the environment. It chose nineteen realized developments and seven that were still in the planning stages as its book went to press. "Celebration is one of the most successful communities based on the principles of the new urbanism," the ULI concluded.

But the ULI made an even more conclusive judgment in October 2001 when it awarded Celebration the organization's prestigious Award for Excellence during its annual meeting in Boston.

"Celebration's developers brought the best minds to the table throughout the community's many years of planning and development," according to ULI jury chairman Robert N. Ruth, who is also senior managing director of the Trammell Crow Company in Torrance, California. "With its emphasis on architectural quality, its careful integration of housing types and land uses, and its ingenious nurturing of institutions and infrastructure—both hard and soft—the community has made meaningful differences in the lives of the people who live there. Celebration has set a benchmark for new community development worldwide," Ruth said.

Celebration is, in fact, so successful that there has been a steady stream of architects, planners, and developers through Celebration. And some one hundred communities are being built around the country that are in some large measure based on the experience of this town.

But the experiment's real success should be measured not in dollars and cents, not in reduced expectations, or even in dreams—realized or thwarted—but in whether the real town of Celebration that exists today in any way resembles the excellent town that was planned. And by that criterion, the town seems to be a winner.

Celebration is beautiful, friendly, clean, efficient, and safe. The quality of life is clearly, by any measure, excellent. But what is most impressive about Celebration is the vigor of the public life here and the level of involvement, not to mention the sheer number of educational, social, cultural, recreational, and volunteer activities available in a town this size—and a seemingly insatiable appetite for ever more activity.

More than all of this, perhaps, is something less tangible but truly eye-opening. And that is the ongoing and mutual nourishing of neighbor for neighbor without regard, as they say, for race, religion, creed, etc. This true neighborliness that puts action into care is indistinguishable from real affection, which many of these people have for each other and for their town.

Celebration is also beginning to be more and more integrated into the Osceola County and greater Orlando areas and to produce necessary links to neighboring Kissimmee and St. Cloud as well as Orlando. And Celebration is starting to produce high-caliber young people who are debating and twirling and golfing in statewide and national arenas. Art, culture, and religion thrive. The work ethic is seriously in play despite the relative financial well-being of the town.

On the other hand, the experience has not been a happy one for some of the original residents of Celebration, who moved in and then moved on to lives elsewhere. Some of those who have remained feel sobered by the early struggles of the town. And, certainly, the high expectations of each and every Celebration pioneer could not possibly have been satisfied. "It's called the Pixie Dust factor," says Bill Bona.

"We take great pride in the success of the community," says Perry Reader, who has overseen the transition of Celebration from a conglomeration of buildings to a living, breathing community, and who has accrued fans and detractors along the way.

Among the new traditions of the town are extensive decorations for all occasions.

The parks and playgrounds dotting Celebration offer dozens of recreational opportunities for children.

New Urbanist pioneer Andrés Duany, who was involved in the early planning stages of Celebration, and whose work certainly inspired the Celebration planners, at least in part, has been generous in his praise of Disney's town, comparing it favorably to his own community, Seaside.

"In the end," Duany suggests, "Celebration should be assessed the way all urbanist development should be assessed—not by photos and short visits, which suffice for architectural criticism, but by inhabiting the place. Does the community improve how a day is lived? Does it accommodate the ebb and flow of life?"

A question that can be answered with a resounding yes!

And in conclusion, Duany wrote in *Urban Land*, the ULI magazine, "Celebration promises to become the most influential new town since Radburn, New Jersey [in 1927]...."

Wrote Michael Pollan, in 1997, "Disney's town has already become what Disney's founder intended—a stop on the architectural tour of the American future."

Still excited about Celebration is the man who is probably most responsible for its creation, Disney CEO Michael Eisner, the man who gave Celebration the green light.

"I believe that the reason Celebration is such a dynamic community today," he said in accepting the ULI award, "is because it began with a dynamic community of planners, designers, and architects, who were determined to create a place that was not just another subdivision."

It seems unlikely that anyone, however they feel about Celebration, would ever represent it as "just another subdivision." Celebration is something entirely new, different, and other. It's a lovely place, and it may have fundamentally affected the way Americans live.

POSTSCRIPT

On the face of it, I was probably not the ideal writer for a book about a small, neotraditional Southern town comprised mainly of young families. As a single, middle-aged modernist who lives in Manhattan, the reality (I should say "realities") of Celebration should have seemed odd, if not downright alien. After all, when I feel a need to "get away from it all," I don't head for a mountain cabin. I fly to Los Angeles, where I lived for fifteen years and still have many friends. (Hi, Ben!)

On the other hand, I have a strong personal interest in history, particularly that of domestic architecture (for the past twelve years I have been an editor at *Metropolitan Home* magazine). And, like many people who have never been to such a place, I share our country's collective nostalgia for Andy and Opie's Mayberry. So I wasn't totally hostile to Celebration, particularly as the town features public buildings by some of America's finest architects.

In fact, my first experience with Celebration was in the fall of 1996, when Disney CEO Michael Eisner hosted all the architects, planners, landscapers, etc., who had designed Celebration, along with selected members of the design and architectural press. Robert A.M. Stern and Jaquelin T. Robertson, whose firms jointly produced the Celebration master plan, took groups of journalists on walking tours of a downtown that still smelled of fresh paint in toy-box colors.

At the time, downtown Celebration consisted of street-level shops and restaurants with apartments upstairs; the AMC movie house; Town Hall; a branch of the U.S. Post Office; and other public buildings, as well as the few homes (including a handful of model homes) that were then complete. That evening, in a vacant lot where the Celebration Hotel now stands, a tent was erected for dinner. It would prove to be my first of many meals in this Central Florida town.

I returned to Celebration in 2003. What I had remembered as a large downtown in the middle of a sprawling construction zone punctuated by a handful of completed houses, I now saw as a tiny town surrounded by neighborhoods shaded by surprisingly mature vegetation. Trees grow fast in the subtropics. The Market Street I remembered was still there, looking as appealing as its opening day, yet I found myself deeply suspicious, and my cynicism began to pester my early fact-finding days in Celebration.

It's pretty, I thought, and clean. Soon I came to add "friendly" to my list of salient characteristics of the place. It seemed safe. The teenagers on skateboards looked scruffy but said things like "excuse me" and "yes, sir," which is not what I am used to in New York City, where teenagers look scruffy and say things that can't be printed here. There weren't many restaurants, but they were all credible (especially Columbia, which I just have to say for the record is my favorite, though I can't really imagine better clam chowder than they serve at the Celebration Town Tavern).

So with all this going for it, my native New York brain kept asking, what's wrong with it? Or at least I wondered until the town began to work its way with me in unexpected ways.

Do I find Celebration artificial? In a way, yes, but no more artificial than other purpose-built communities. And probably not more artificial than I might have found Savannah five minutes after all those lovely residential squares were put in.

Did the retro architecture bother me? Well, as a dedicated modernist, it did at first. But it's certainly better looking and less contrived than many a "modern" community—like the generic subdivisions of Valencia that grew up around California Institute of the Arts, where I studied and later taught. (If you've seen *E.T.*, you've seen the kind of place I'm talking about.) Given a choice between Celebration and New Hyde Park, the Long Island town in which I spent my childhood— a post–World War II, Levitt-inspired housing development—I'd be moving south.

Did I find Celebration visually conformist? In fact, I had the opposite reaction. Sure, there was a certain similarity to the houses, all of which have architectural details that predate my birth, which was not recent. But there is also far more variety in the homes— both in their design and their size—than there is in Valencia or New Hyde Park. In fact, in its diversity, Celebration most resembles the small, nineteenth-century town of Hamilton, New York, home to Colgate University, where I was an undergraduate, and the residential neighborhoods of eighteenth-century New Haven, Connecticut, where I lived during graduate school at Yale.

Finally, what won me over—in a big way—was the sense of community and the enormous energy for good that motivates the population of this town. The people who live in Celebration are better educated and more articulate, I suspect, than any comparable group of adults anywhere. They have a seemingly limitless appetite for socializing, organizing, and volunteering. *What do you need?* Everyone seems to be thinking on a nonstop basis, *And how can we meet that need and turn it into a fund-raiser for some good cause at the same time?*

There is a fairly broad range of people living in Celebration, but there are common threads. The people who took the chance to live here care deeply about their families, that's clear, but they care almost equally as much about each other and about creating and maintaining a real community that doesn't pretend to be utopian. It's just a place where decent people are trying to allow each other to be the best of themselves. And they are very, very kind to strangers.

I found myself enjoying the town enormously. I liked beginning to know the cast of characters (large but finite). I came to know certain restaurant servers and shopkeepers by name—along with the names of their spouses and children and their best friends—more than I thought I could ever retain of their individual biographies. I knew that some of the breakfast regulars at the Market Street Café would be absent on Friday because they'd be at the Rotary Club meeting, which is held at the Seasons cafeteria at Celebration Health, about ten minutes after dawn.

I began to learn the routines and rituals of the town and started to know who lived where and when they moved in. I could get around without thinking, in a car, on foot, or driving a NEV. I had favorite meals at each of the town's eateries, and knew where to get the things I needed. I was surprised to find myself missing Celebration within days of each return to New York, and I was eager, each time, to return—as I am now, writing this in the arctic chill of New York in February. The Hudson River may be a lot bigger than the Town Center Lake, but I suspect that Town Center Lake doesn't ever freeze.

So, yes, like so many people who come to Celebration on purpose or by accident, I tried to wrap my reality around the possibility of buying into Celebration. And part of me is frankly sad that it just doesn't seem feasible.

So my thanks to the people of Celebration, who put out their communal welcome mat for me. And for the lessons of mutual respect they have taught me. And for the stories of care and tolerance I have heard from those who have been shown kindness and acceptance. Although they love the familiar, the citizens of Celebration don't seem to have any particular fear of difference. Indeed, the town takes pride in its growing heterogeneity and looks forward to even greater diversity in the future.

I have even been known to say that if you don't like Celebration, you just haven't been there long enough.

By way of closing, I'd like to reprint the following from *An American Celebration*, the Celebration Women's Club cookbook, an entry by real estate broker Pattie Gaw:

Our Recipe for Celebration

> *1 caring group of people*
> *1 beautiful Florida community*
> ADD:
> *2 cups of happiness*
> *3 quarts of fun*
> *Limitless patience*
> *A pinch of humor*
> MIX WITH:
> 2,000 families of every kind
> Blend thoughtfully
> Create a loving town
> To be served with a warm smile

Now this is the kind of thing that I might once have dismissed (in my "contempt prior to investigation" days). But reading it after having spent some time in Celebration (and having actually met the ebullient and down-to-earth Pattie Gaw, who resembles a younger, peppier, more American Jeanne Moreau), I have to say it's more than a little accurate.

I've come to think of Celebration as a personal haven and maybe a new part of the world that feels in some way like home. And if that seems corny, well, so be it. As Walt Disney himself used to say:

"All right, I'm corny. But I think there's just about a hundred and forty million people in this country who are just as corny as I am."

INDEX

Page numbers in *italics* refer to photographs.

ACKNOWLEDGMENTS

I'd like to thank the good men and women of The Celebration Company who introduced me to the town: the vivacious Andrea Finger (luv huh!), Matt Kelly, Kimberly Locher, Mike Mekdeci, Barbara Muenks, and the effusive Marilyn Waters especially (say hi to Wing for me).

My thanks, too, to Pat Wasson, the hardworking but cheerful executive director of Town Hall and something of the town's mayor. I also want to thank Michael Eisner, Jaquelin T. Robertson, and Robert A.M. Stern for their insights (also Peter Dixon of the Stern office and Ed Siegel of Cooper Robertson). I am grateful, too, to those former Disney executives who gave so generously of their time to talk once again about the early days, in particular Peter Rummell and Todd Mansfield. My thanks, too, to Disney Imagineering's Wing Chao, whom I just have to say, I find to be one of the loveliest people I've ever met (not to mention a prodigious talent with daunting credentials).

I would like to thank Katherine and Richard Greene, whom I have never met, but who were more than generous in any case, offering up the fruits of their labors for me to purloin. For a highly personal, inside look at the life of Walt Disney, I recommend their book, *Inside the Dream*, as well as the documentary film the book is based on, *Walt, the Man Behind the Myth*, which is, of course, available on DVD.

I also want to thank the ever-supportive and probably miraculous Wendy Lefkon, my editor at Disney Editions, for her ongoing faith in me—not to mention her friendship and lunches at the Mesa Grill. Thanks to Marsha Melnick of Roundtable Press, for keeping me focused, and with good will and humor, and whose editorial help was much appreciated; and thanks to John Glenn, also of Roundtable, for his insights, editorial emendations, research skills, and efficient handling of many necessary tasks. I thank, too, the talented Jon Glick, the book's designer, for this, our second entirely pleasant collaboration.

Thanks, too, to all the photographers whose work appears in these pages, but particularly to Mark Ashman and Gary Bogdon, who made the town come alive in their "day in the life of" photos of the people of Celebration. And if there is anyone I have omitted, I thank you in my heart even if my diminishing memory seems to have excluded you here.

I'd also like to thank my parents—again—this time for making family life so central a part of my upbringing, and the neighbors of my childhood: the Cosgroves, Kruks, Levines, LoPrestis, Perlmans, Thieses, Pancamos, LaFeminas, Sternbergs, Schmidts, and, of course, the Ekblads, family friends for a lifetime. We had a neighborhood despite the odds against it.

I also want to express my gratitude to the residents of Celebration. You really did make me feel welcome in your town and in your homes. To those who had the courage to be critical of Celebration, in the past and present tense, even though you thought you would be ignored: I promise you, even if your concerns do not appear in this book, I heard you and respect you enormously.

I would also like to thank the following Celebrants by name for their time, candor, and hospitality: Claudine Andrews and Keith Albrizzi; Lisa Baird; Lyn and David Berelsman; Bill and Susan Bona; Susan Brasfield; Becky and Sonny Buoncervello; John Bushey; Patrick Carrin; Heather Clayton; Ron Clifton; John and Teresa Conroy; Paul Cooney; Sarai Cowin; Des Cummings; Joe Davison; Jim Doran; Jan and Charlie Eldredge; Scott Fought; Pattie and Mike Gaw; Linda Goodwin-Nichols; Maria Grulich; all the Habers (Terri, Larry, Brandon, and Staci); Kathy and Jim Hattaway; JoAnn Hudson; Darlene and Randy Johnson; Dorothy Johnson; Mark Jones: Christine and Tod Joossens; Steve Katz; Mary Ann Kinser; Brian Levine; Don McDonald; Alex Morton; Gary Moyer; Peg and Rod Owens; Sonny Patel; Mary Pfeiffer; Vicki Puntonet; Dick Rianhard; Mark Robinson; Charlie Rogers; Lynn Sands; Dawn Thomas; Lorraine and Mike Turner; John Van Fossen; Hank and Mary Wake; Rob Wight; and Patrick Wrisley.

I have to acknowledge, too, the members of the Architectural Review Committee for letting me sit in on their meeting, and the CROA board and the planning committee of the American Cancer Society's Relay for Life, for the same reason. A great big shout-out goes to all the giddy geriatrics at the Celebrators Happy Hour—you folks throw a swell party! And a special thank-you to the Rotarians of Celebration, for your warm welcome and, of course, for letting me keep the cash I won in the raffle (I did, as promised, spend it in Celebration). My thanks, too, to the congregation of the Community Presbyterian Church—it was a joy to worship with you. Much appreciation, too, to the highly professional waiters and waitresses of every eatery in town for putting up with my taping at breakfast, brunch, elevenses, lunch, coffee break, high tea, dinner, and nightcap. And much appreciation goes to everyone who let us photograph them going about their private and public lives.

Last, but by no means least, I would like to thank Perry Reader, the now-retired president of The Celebration Company. He's a highly congenial breakfast date, which is high praise from someone who is not usually awake for breakfast by any normal definition of the word. Without Perry Reader, this book—and much of what is good about Celebration—would not have happened. Godspeed, Perry!

—MICHAEL LASSELL

New York City,
February 2004